This careful collection gives the r
the lives of migrants, the people they find along their journeys
and the worlds they inevitably create together. It also conveys
the complexity and contradictions of experiences of migration
and makes plain that these experiences are inseparable from
personal and political belonging, and perhaps even what it
means to be human. From its incisive introductory chapter, this
'unapologetically local' book nonetheless imparts important
lessons for a global audience, from the expert to the casual
reader, on how people make sense of movement – theirs or that
of others – within and across borders.

E Tendayi Achiume, United Nations Special Rapporteur
on racism, racial discrimination, xenophobia
and related intolerance

Like all excellent ideas, the one that animates this book is both
disarmingly simple and powerfully original. So much has been
written on xenophobia in South Africa, and yet so few have
listened with care and precision to the voices of the ordinary
people at the coalface. This book unsettles so many old
assumptions, like who is host and who visitor, who belongs and
what indeed it might mean to belong at all. It does this simply
by creating a space in which people bear witness to their lives.

Jonny Steinberg, Professor of African Studies,
Oxford University and author of A Man of Good Hope

These are raw, honest, personal stories – some heart-breaking,
some up-lifting. All creatively collected and beautifully told.
Each story is a study in journey-making. No matter where
we may have been born, each of us seeks a place where we
will be safe and respected for who we are. The stories in this
collection illustrate that no journey is easy – each act of leaving
and each attempt to begin again is tough. At their core however,

these stories grapple with the making of a nation. They teach us about urban poverty and women's struggles for space and freedom and of course they speak of racism. Taken together, these narratives illustrate the quest for dignity and so they tell the story of humanity and striving and ambition in the midst of profound difficulty. This book speaks to South African and African concerns but at its heart, it documents a set of global phenomena that are important to anyone who cares about the state of the world today.

Sisonke Msimang, activist and author of
Always Another Country

I WANT TO GO HOME FOREVER

I WANT TO GO HOME FOREVER

STORIES OF BECOMING AND BELONGING
IN SOUTH AFRICA'S GREAT METROPOLIS

EDITED BY

LOREN B LANDAU AND TANYA PAMPALONE

WITS UNIVERSITY PRESS

Published in South Africa by:
Wits University Press
1 Jan Smuts Avenue
Johannesburg, 2001

www.witspress.co.za

First published 2018

http://dx.doi.org.10.18772/22018082217

978-1-77614-221-7 (Print)
978-1-77614-222-4 (Web PDF)
978-1-77614-231-6 (EPUB)

Project manager: Inga Norenius
Copy editor: Inga Norenius
Proofreader: Danya Ristić-Schacherl
Cover and book design: Peter Bosman Design
Cover artwork: Senzo Shabangu
Maps: Miriam Maina, redrawn by Jabedi Maps
Photographs: Madelene Cronje, Mark Lewis and Oupa Nkosi
Typesetter: Newgen
Typeset in 10.5 point Sabon

We are deeply grateful for a Constitution that encompasses all that is good in us and a constitutional order that protects our hard-won freedom. Mindful of our gains, we nevertheless know that a long, long road lies ahead, with many twists and turns, sometimes through difficult and trying times. Poverty, ill health and hunger still stalk our land. Greed and avarice show their ugly faces. Xenophobia and intolerance play their mischief in our beautiful land.

AHMED KATHRADA, SPEAKING AT NELSON MANDELA'S FUNERAL IN QUNU, EASTERN CAPE, DECEMBER 2015

Contents

* Not the narrator's real name

Foreword

I have a deep, personal connection with migration. My parents met in Bloemfontein during apartheid. They were from a different province, migrant workers living as 'foreigners' in the Free State, given the influx control laws of the time. Soon after I was born, our small family moved to Mmabatho, in the bantustan state of Bophuthatswana. In 1988, when I was seven, political strife forced us to flee to Botswana. During the process of moving, my father, sister and grandmother nearly died in a car accident that took place under mysterious circumstances, so we continued to live with fear and insecurity. My father wouldn't say why, but it had to do with Lucas Mangope, the president of Bophuthatswana. The Anglican Church ended up giving my father a job and providing comfortable shelter and school for my sister and me in Botswana. My parents always told us that one day, we would go back home to South Africa.

When my baby sister and I started at our new school, it wasn't easy to explain where exactly we came from. For her, it didn't really matter because five-year-olds have little awareness of such things and adapt easily. I, however, was still traumatised by the car accident and, although I was little, I knew exactly what was going on. I also knew it was not likely that I would ever see my friends and old teachers again. It's bad enough being the new kid in school, but having a weird back story makes you stick out even more. Eventually I found my way; my school had children from all over the world, and the South African community in Gaborone was closely involved with the Anglican Church, which played a significant role in the anti-apartheid movement. Looking back, I am grateful that I had a strong, caring community to buffer me from the sense of alienation that typifies the experiences of many migrants across Africa. Also, my family remained intact and we were comforted and fortified by the love and protection of our parents.

During quiet time at home, my parents would tell us stories about South Africa, insisting that we came from a country of brave and talented people, and it was to South Africa that we belonged. They would play songs that were banned at home, by musicians like Miriam Makeba and Hugh Masekela. My father had a personal connection with the latter because they attended the same school and the story of Sophiatown tied in with their respective lives. My father had begun his priesthood there, in the township made famous by the forced removals of 1956, which split up the multiracial community and relocated families to Soweto and other areas. His political awareness and quiet activism began during those years. When my parents told us about the Soweto riots of 1976, my mother would relate how they started outside Morris Isaacson, the high school where she was working as a maths student teacher. It wasn't long after that she left for Bloemfontein – a safer and more stable environment – to study nursing. Around the same time my father also relocated to Bloemfontein from Soweto for similar reasons. Even before I was born, my parents had to migrate from the places that they knew as home.

After ten relatively happy years in Botswana, it was time to go back. South Africa was now a democratic state and our lives were no longer in danger. I was well integrated in Botswana, with a strong friendship circle and a flourishing academic life. My father was given a parish to lead in the sleepy, tiny gold-mining town of Stilfontein in North West province. I had been looking forward to coming home but the culture shock was too much for me to handle. It was a closed society with high racial tensions and my new school was as different from my old school as it could have been. The students were lukewarm, although friendly, but they were also curious about me, which caused me great discomfort. When it was time to go to university, I went to Pretoria, which seemed to be simply a metropolitan version of Stilfontein – Afrikaans, exclusive and hostile. The continuing culture shock was so intense that I succumbed to a deep depression. I had to escape and eventually found Johannesburg, the city of dreams and diversity. Acclimatising to life here was very easy; I found a home among artists and intellectuals from South Africa and around the world. I can confidently say that I am finally home.

This is my story, one that I often tell when people ask, as they often do, 'Where are you from?' Johannesburg is characterised by its local and transnational migrant population and it is not unique among other major global cities in this regard. But the stories that this city's migrants have to tell are as varied as the places from which they hail.

Stories are a powerful tool to help us understand individuals and society. People's stories matter; they are how we make meaning of life, organise views of ourselves and others, make decisions and justify them and understand our place in the world. We live in a world where we talk about our lives. When we tell our stories ourselves, rather than have them told by others, we maintain personal agency and therefore our dignity. I have no shame in my story because I am the one relating it and choose what to share and with whom. Stories in the first person can more easily inspire us to think about the social integration of migrants, and also help us to define a moral ground that will guide us in addressing their needs from a human perspective.

Like many small-town children, I spent a lot of my time fantasising about living in Johannesburg. After all, this is a city of opportunity, where with a bit of luck and hard work, people can make a good life for themselves. Some people come to work and send remittances to their home countries, while others come in the hopes of striking the proverbial gold. This is exemplified in this collection by a Mozambican migrant, Lucas Machel, who tells Oupa Nkosi how his father supported his family by working in the gold mines. Machel follows in his footsteps by relocating to Johannesburg to take care of his young family back home. In true Joburg style, he goes on the hustle, from working at a farm to making his living as a bricklayer. He insists, however, that this kind of life is temporary and he aims to retire back home in Mozambique.

One of the distinctive features of contemporary migration is sex work. Esther Khumalo is a Zimbabwean who works in the streets of the central business district (CBD) of Johannesburg. She lays bare the plight of migrant sex workers by sharing her experiences of sexual violence and limited access to medication due to her undocumented status and the xenophobia of healthcare workers.

Refugees also face challenges that are brought into stark relief in two poignant narrations by Estifanos Worku Abeto from Ethiopia and Alphonse Nahimana from Rwanda. Their experiences highlight pre-migration trauma, post-migration difficulties and the need for social support for migrants. South Africa has one of the highest numbers of unsettled asylum seekers in the world, and resettlement is often difficult for them because of the deep flaws that exist in the immigration system. This imperils their safety, economic security and social integration. Abeto finds it difficult to integrate into society because of his asylum status even though he would like to make a contribution by assisting other refugees. Nahimana's flight from Rwanda underscores how asylum seekers carry their trauma with them and do not find the mental health resources to help them recover. Narrating his experiences is a way of Nahimana taking on his trauma, and for him, storytelling is an effective coping mechanism.

This book would not be complete without a couple of love stories. Azam Khan comes from Pakistan where, as a restless youth, he is told about opportunities to make money in South Africa. He finds success in Pretoria but blows his cash due to a financially reckless lifestyle and has to start all over again. This humbling experience finds Khan selling merchandise from door to door, and it's during one of these sales visits that he meets the woman whom he goes on to marry. She is from the local township and, due to cultural differences, her family is not quick to accept him. However, Khan manages to integrate and gains the confidence of his love's family and community. This is not the only story about finding love away from home; there is also a touching narration about how two Nigerians meet and go on to make a life together in a foreign land.

Personal connections aside, I believe *I Want to Go Home Forever* will resonate with all readers because, after all, we are a migratory species. Starting from the Cradle of Humankind, we have moved over the years and gone on to populate our entire planet. Stories about migration are more than just about changes in geography; they are about factors that drive us to survive and find our own corner in the world, however temporary, where we can make a meaningful life for ourselves. That is worth writing home about!

KARABO K KGOLENG
JOHANNESBURG, MAY 2018

Preface

All books are collective endeavours, this collection perhaps more than most. Although we, as editors, conceptualised the text and shepherded its production, few of the words within these covers are our own. In contemporary urban studies, cities are often described as co-productions: the result of interactions among officials and residents, developers, global economic conditions and even meteorological forces. While weather played a minimal role, this text is undeniably the result of many hands and voices. Without the narrators who told their stories and the writers who captured them, it would not exist. Only their dedication and diversity – linguistic, legal, national, class, professional, political – allowed us to compile these stories. There are undoubtedly still gaps; voices and perspectives that remain missing. Despite the book's undeniable shortcomings and silences, we must not underestimate the importance of sharing these accounts.

There are a number of other people and institutions who offered this project their witting and unwitting support as well. First among these is South Africa's National Research Foundation. Through their research chair initiative, we garnered the financial support needed to undertake a project with no immediate practical benefits. We are grateful for the opportunity this gave us to reflect so critically and creatively on what South Africa is and what it is becoming. The University of the Witwatersrand provided further in-kind support and an institutional home for our motley crew. Wits University Press – particularly Roshan Cader, Andrew Joseph and Inga Norenius – have provided invaluable support in realising this book. We would like to thank Karabo Kgoleng for her thoughtful and generous foreword, and artist Senzo Shabangu, whose own work continuously tackles issues of migration and a search for home, for allowing us to use his image on the cover of this collection. We must also flag the important contributions made by Emma Monama, who helped navigate the university's somewhat byzantine administrative systems in ways which enabled our narrators and writers to get the resources required to complete the project. As a street-smart South African, she also proved indispensable in compiling the glossary of local terms and places. Lenore Longwe, as is her wont, provided logistical support and warm-hearted administrative advice. Kabiri Bule assembled the timeline, which helps situate the people and processes the following pages describe. Barbara Ludman and Aneesa Fazel reviewed the copy before submission and provided essential feedback. The maps were designed initially by Miriam Maina on only a handshake and the promise of a bottle of gin. That original bottle may be long gone but we hope that as this book goes to print she and all the others who made this book possible will join us in toasting its completion.

LOREN B LANDAU AND TANYA PAMPALONE
JOHANNESBURG, FEBRUARY 2018

Maps

MAP 1: Journeys to Gauteng

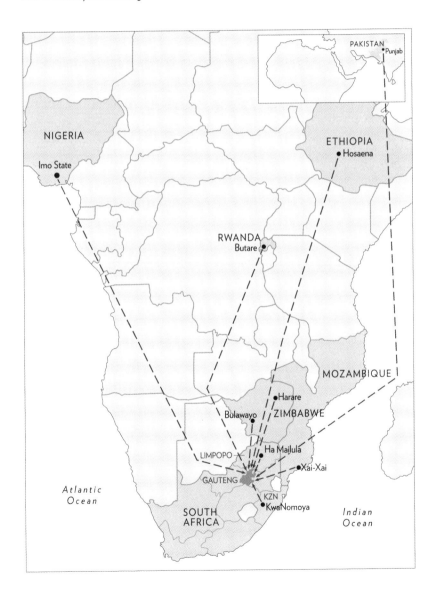

MAP 2: Gauteng province and surroundings

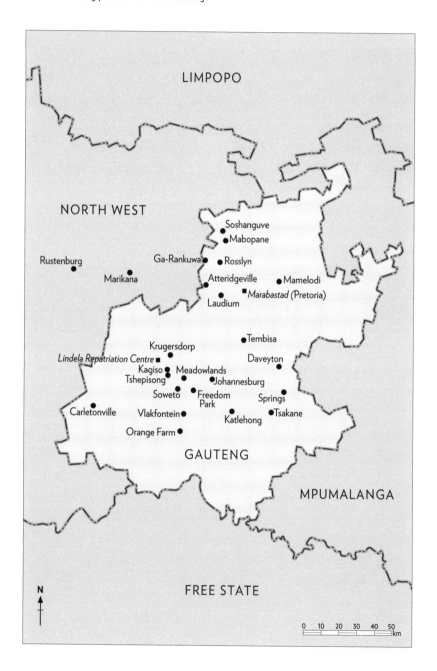

MAP 3: Central Gauteng

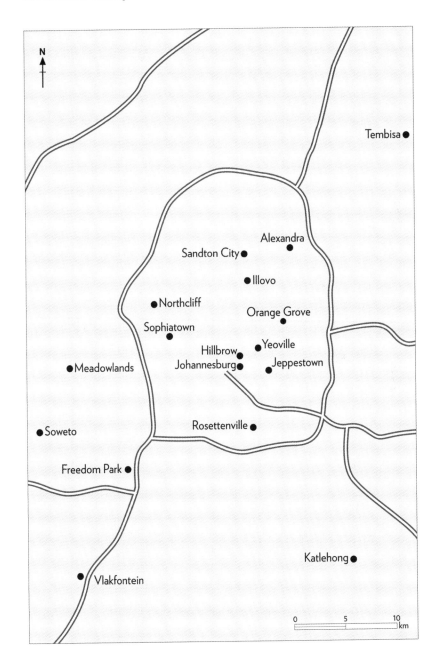

Introduction

It has been a bit more than two decades since apartheid gave way to democracy and the buildings that house the Constitutional Court look worn. The expressions boldly inscribed on the walls in South Africa's 11 official languages – words pledging, among other constitutional commitments, that the country 'belongs to all who live in it, united in our diversity' – are fading under the fierce Highveld sun. Some letters are missing, likely pried from their surface to sell as scrap metal alongside many of the city's manhole covers.

In its former life, the court was an imposing military fort and prison where apartheid's antagonists were detained and tortured. Now, from its hilltop perch in the heart of Johannesburg, Constitution Hill overlooks a place of promise: the noisy, dynamic, sometimes dangerous downtown centre of Hillbrow, an unwitting symbol of South Africa's transformation. Once a gateway for European immigrants, today the neighbourhood is home to migrants from the country's nine provinces and the continent's almost countless countries. People converge on the streets at all hours – an exception in a city where many residents lock themselves behind metal gates, electrified fences and razor wire-topped walls before the sun sets. It is a place feared by many, wealthy or poor, white or black. It has become a metonym for all the dangers many believe immigrants import into the country: drugs, violence, prostitution, degradation, lawlessness, corruption. But it is also where tomato sellers and labourers share the streets with students, children and hustlers trying to feed their families and their aspirations.

Just 50 kilometres to the north is Pretoria, apartheid's former political nerve centre. It too is being transformed by people from across the country and the continent. Whether in the inner city, Sunnyside, or the townships of Soshanguve or Mamelodi, South

African migrants live and work side by side with long-term residents and new, international arrivals. Together Pretoria, Johannesburg and the municipalities surrounding them make up the Gauteng City Region, a mega-city positioning itself as the economic pulse of Africa, abounding with promise and opportunity.

For authorities, the arrival of immigrants and migrants often threatens their hopes for a prosperous, orderly 'world class African city' – the marketing tagline once adopted by the City of Johannesburg. At the forefront of the current backlash is Johannesburg's mayor, the Democratic Alliance's Herman Mashaba. A pull-himself-up-by-the-bootstraps businessman, he took over running the city from the African National Congress (ANC) after the 2016 local elections. He finds a fraternal spirit in Solly Msimanga, Pretoria's mayor, elected on promises to clean up the city and reclaim neighbourhoods lost to 'crime and grime'.

From his office just blocks away from the Constitutional Court, Mashaba marked his first 100 days in office by telling journalists that illegal immigrants were 'holding our country to ransom' and that he was 'going to be the last South African to allow it'. Just a few months later the City of Pretoria approved what the Mamelodi Concerned Residents coalition called an 'anti-foreigner march', protesting against foreigners whom they blamed for bringing drugs, prostitution and joblessness to their communities. Such official rhetoric and community actions reflect an intensification of the ANC government's urban clean-up interventions and increasingly nationalist politics. For almost two decades, Gauteng's cities have been the target of interventions to reclaim the country's premier urban space. Ostensibly going after gangsters who sell drugs and sex or have hijacked buildings, the government has used the combined power of police, immigration officials and private security to evict and arrest many of the neighbourhoods' poor – often foreign – residents.

It is easy to condemn politicians' populism as an exclusive nationalism that contradicts the South African Constitution's post-apartheid inclusivity. Yet for many South Africans, the constitutional promises of freedom have given way to civilian death rates higher than some active war zones. Institutionalised racism and spatial segregation continue, while adequate healthcare and quality education remain fantasies. Economic inequality has worsened in the democratic era and formal job opportunities for black South Africans have declined. In navigating these disappointments, cohesion often gives way to discrimination and conflict. Marginalised citizens' struggles for economic rights have taken many forms, and all too often these frustrations fuel the demonisation of migrants and their violent exclusion. Foreigners often bear the brunt, but South Africans deemed too dark, foreign-looking or from the 'wrong' group also face their neighbours' contempt.

It is into the spaces among these groups that we venture.

Through the oral histories of 13 Gauteng residents – six foreign, the others South African – we go beyond statistics, established discourses, existing literature and accepted narratives. We get to know the insider and the outsider, though it is not always clear who is who in spaces where almost everyone is from somewhere else. We aim to capture the emotions and relations that emerge from the space between outrage and hope, the making of selves and the other, as people confront the loss of a longed-for future. In so doing, this book tells stories of both violence and solidarity. Of leaving and coming. Of becoming.

Some of those from beyond South Africa's borders are fleeing persecution in their homeland. Some seek respite from broken relationships. Many others are simply looking for ways of escaping poverty. All seek opportunities – profit, protection or passage elsewhere – in South Africa. The responses of those born within South Africa's borders veer widely, from working to shape a secure future by incorporating newcomers into an ever-changing population, to turning their frustration and activism against outsiders. For some, the violence they endorse is rooted in deep commitments to realising the rights for which black South Africans have long struggled. For others, the violence reflects a fundamental betrayal of the South Africa they still hope to build.

The stories collected here are but a few that could be told of the millions who have moved to, through or within South Africa in the past decades. Of those, there are roughly two million foreigners now living among the country's 55 million residents. Of Gauteng's 12 million people, almost ten per cent are foreign born. Yet there are many more migrant stories to tell. Almost 35 per cent of the province's population has come from elsewhere in the country. Living amongst them are those who have only journeyed across time, who have spent their lives in Gauteng while the country's politics has changed around them. All, no matter their citizenship, face similar forms of marginalisation and social discrimination. Together they transform both themselves and Gauteng and in the process they are mapping South Africa's future.

WAYS OF TELLING

In May 2008, Estifanos Worku Abeto was living in a refugee camp in Springs, a small town 50 kilometres east of Johannesburg. Bright white United Nations tents formed neat aisles on a parched lot alongside a main road, brittle winds scraping the dirt and snapping at the temporary shelters. Those who had been chased from their homes in the massive outbreak of violence against foreigners huddled in tents with their families or set up makeshift stoeps and spoke with their new neighbours. Worku Abeto struck a more solitary figure. He wore a heavy coat and a long face and gripped a Bible.

Like many other journalists in Gauteng at the time, Tanya Pampalone, joined by photographer Sally Shorkend, travelled to the various camps that had been set up in Johannesburg and Pretoria, speaking to more than a dozen people who had fled from their homes, recording their stories in words and images. As Tanya recalls, 'We did what journalists do for this sort of piece: show up at a place, talk to people, take down their words, go back to the office, transform the conversations into a story and insert images which help show what words never can. We did not expect to see Worku Abeto – or the others we had met during those disturbing weeks – again.'

Globally, this is how the media tends to cover migrancy and violence: as events. Journalists take down the story as it combusts, showing disturbing images of children lying lifeless on beaches, of capsized boats, of refugee camps that stretch for kilometres across hopeless landscapes. Readers lament over the inhumanity of what is in fact human; shocked, saddened, disturbed, each time. In South Africa, too, we have watched the bodies, the burning, the lives destroyed and the lives lost, and we shame those who have inflicted it. How can we do this to our African neighbours? And when people say they reject *kwerekweres* in their neighbourhoods, in their country, we forget to listen to what else is being said. We forget to understand. We forget; we move on; we wait until the next event, the next combustion.

Academics are little better. In South Africa, studies of migration focus largely on the legacies of labour migration or the need to recruit highly skilled professionals to help run the country's service sector and industries. Even scholars dedicated to improving services or urban planning often overlook just how fragmented and mobile South Africa's population is. Globally, scholars of international migration and, particularly, of displacement, tend to focus on questions of victimisation. Few studies speak about the migrants' own role in violence, oppression and persecution. Jonny Steinberg's *A Man of Good Hope*, which traces the story of Asad Abdullahi, a Somali immigrant to South Africa, and Dave Eggers's story of Valentino Achak Deng in *What Is the What*, are rare exceptions in this regard. Recognising that migrants are actors and agents takes nothing away from the victimisation they face – the rights violations and economic deprivation that motivated their move. But seeing migrants as capable of duplicity and manipulation is to see them as human, capable of shaping themselves and – by accident or design – the world around them.

Since the mid-1990s, the African Centre for Migration & Society, where Loren B Landau is based, has sought to deepen understandings of mobility and its intersection with South Africa's broader transformation and the country's relationships beyond its borders. To complicate narratives of mobility and difference in the country, in 2013 we, the two editors of this book, collaborated on *Writing Invisibility: Conversations on the Hidden City*, a collection of stories on urban migrancy published by the *Mail & Guardian*. Over the years, we had spoken about the *Voice of Witness* book series, created by Eggers to help tell stories of marginalised people who are often spoken about but rarely offered the chance to speak in their own words. This book, like his series, is based on the belief that recounting these stories to the broader readership is in its small way humanising, liberatory and subversive. Inspired by the series, we had been kicking around the idea of oral histories anchored around migrancy and xenophobia in South Africa. Following the success of *Writing Invisibility,* we decided to take the leap.

BOILING POINTS

As the timeline at the end of this book shows, South Africa's entangled history of xenophobia reaches deep and wide throughout the making of the nation. Most of this book's stories, however, play out against a backdrop of anti-outsider violence that began in May 2008.

At the start of that cold winter, with the ruling ANC in disarray, Mozambican national Ernesto Alfabeto Nhamuave was set alight in Alexandra, one of Johannesburg's oldest townships, and images of his charred, enflamed body were broadcast into homes around the world. The 'Burning Man', as the 35-year-old longtime resident of Alex became known, had worked in South Africa for years to support his family back home in rural Mozambique. Despite scores of eyewitnesses, no one was ever charged with his murder. His death and the subsequent judicial response symbolised an episode of violence that awakened many South Africans to vexing questions of immigration, diversity and xenophobia.

Nhamuave's brutal death triggered weeks of violence that quickly spread across Gauteng, and on to informal settlements and townships in KwaZulu-Natal and the Western Cape. According to a 2009 report by the South African Human Rights Commission, the violence ultimately resulted in more than 60 murders, with 700 people wounded, dozens raped and over 100 000 displaced. Along the way, perpetrators razed hundreds of homes and destroyed or redistributed millions of rands' worth of goods. In almost all cases the violence was instigated by people living near or among the victims – South African citizens determined to rid their communities of unwanted intruders.

While most victims were from beyond South Africa's borders, a third of those killed were South Africans who had married foreigners, those who refused to participate in the violent debauchery or those who simply had the misfortune of belonging to groups others considered unworthy of a place in their neighbourhood. After offering unheeded appeals for calm, the government deployed the armed forces and the military entered townships in Gauteng and the Western Cape for the first time since the end of apartheid, containing the violence with overwhelming force. But by the time they arrived, most offending outsiders had already been cleansed from their hostile communities and the belligerents silently slipped away, leaving behind camps filled with tens of thousands of displaced people like Worku Abeto. It took months for the temporary shelters to be emptied and removed.

Official responses to the 2008 attacks were confused, contradictory and often overtly ideological.

During the violence, the government first denied the crisis. Minister of Safety and Security Charles Nqakula initially responded to the attacks in Alexandra by telling the *Pretoria News*: 'It is only a problem, but if it were a crisis, it would be happening right across the country.' After it spread, he and other officials blamed criminal elements, opposition parties and 'sinister forces', occasionally crediting a mysterious 'third force', evoking the hidden hand of white rule in the violence that marked apartheid's dying days. Ronnie Kasrils, who was the minister for intelligence services at the time of the attacks, later admitted these accusations were misguided, although some within government continued to blame criminals and foreigners for instigating the violence. A statement reflecting the official government position, issued on 29 May 2013, noted that 'Cabinet is cautious not to label this violence as xenophobia because preliminary evidence indicates that these acts may be driven primarily by criminality'.

Even as late as May 2017, former South African president Thabo Mbeki – under whose watch the violence spread nationwide – continued to credit 'township thuggery' for the attacks, according to an account of a meeting on African self-governance, published on *IOL*, by Adekeye Adebajo, the director of the Institute for Pan-African Thought and Conversation. Regardless of the stance of government officials, statements from perpetrators and ordinary township residents made it clear that the impetus for the violence was their own. In the words of one Alexandra resident interviewed by *The Times* soon after the 2008 attacks: 'We are not trying to kill anyone but rather solving the problems of our own country. The government is not doing anything about this, so I support what the mob is doing to get rid of foreigners in our country.'

These were not random acts of criminality or spontaneous protest, but violence targeted at demons within, people whose presence came to be seen as an existential threat to South Africa's collective transformation and renaissance. It is not surprising that sporadic attacks continued, with xenophobic violence – together with other forms of violent protest – on a slow boil. But it would be a further seven years before another wave of xenophobic violence hit the country.

In January 2015, the murder of 14-year-old Siphiwe Mahori in Snake Park, Soweto, by a Somalian shopkeeper, sparked another major violent wave targeted against foreigners. It is Mahori's tragic story, told through his mother, Nombuyiselo Ntlane, which begins this collection.

The attacks were further inflamed in March that year, after Zulu King Goodwill Zwelithini told an assembled crowd in Pongola that that it was time to 'get our house in order and clean our land of lice'. The speech read, in part: 'We need to remove all itching bedbugs and lay them bare in the sun; they will choose to hide because of the heat of the sun. We request that all foreigners should take their baggage and be sent back.'

Once again, violence spilled onto Johannesburg's streets with gangs pouring from single-sex dormitories, incinerating and looting scores of shops.

At the time of writing in 2018, as South Africa passed the ten-year anniversary of the initial attacks, similar attacks continue and little has been done to calm the undercurrent of frustrated aspirations that caused hundreds of people to lose their lives and livelihoods because they spoke the wrong language, came from the wrong place or were seen as threatening the aspirations of others.

GAUTENG AND THE MAKING OF A NATION

While the book tells stories of migration and xenophobic violence, it is also an account of longing and loss. In the 1972 surrealist classic, *Invisible Cities*, Italo Calvino writes, 'The metropolis has the added attraction that, through what it has become, one can look back with nostalgia at what it was.' Yet few of the narrators on these pages are nostalgic for the massive indignities that they and their families faced under apartheid. Few mourn the forbidden and forbidding cities that lay at the heart of apartheid power, cities designed to reinforce white privilege while the country's black majority – effectively stateless aliens in the land of their birth – were condemned to live in backyard shacks or in the impoverished townships built on white cities' peripheries. Of all the narrators we spoke with, only the induna, Manyathela Mvelase, laments his loss of status that democracy delivered into his world.

But it is not primarily for their pasts that our narrators grieve. Almost all of the voices included in this account reflect nostalgia for futures lost. For the South Africans it is for the promises of 1994's liberation and the possibility of overcoming the inequalities, insecurities and injustices of colonialism and apartheid. For those from beyond its borders, South Africa's wealth and relative stability fuelled hopes of profits, of protection from violence and persecution, or the possibility of passages elsewhere. For foreigners and South Africans alike, Gauteng is the site in which they hoped to realise these dreams. As the province readily boasts on its official website, Gauteng and the global city region it contains is the wealthiest chunk of land in sub-Saharan Africa, responsible for generating approximately ten per cent of the entire continent's GDP.

But like all places of promise, Gauteng represents a site of disappointment and deferral: of individual, familial and national goals once glimpsed that are now seemingly beyond reach. It is a site of deceptions by spouses and siblings, by friends and compatriots and by politicians and political parties. The stories echo with broken promises that the violence and economic deprivations of the past might be overcome, that addressing the rights violations of the past could offer pathways to social status and prosperity.

Yet, for all the disappointment infusing these narratives, they remain stories of creation.

As AbdouMaliq Simone and Graeme Götz note in *Emerging Johannesburg*, Gauteng offers a place of becoming, a site where people can discover in themselves sources of resilience and resentment, of confusion and direction. As these individual experiences collide and converge in Gauteng, they are doing more than reshaping individuals: they are remaking the province. The telling of foreign stories alternating with South Africans' stories thus creates a larger story of co-production, of making a present and futures, and simultaneously making a place – the great metropolis of Gauteng.

By bringing together people from across the country, the continent and elsewhere in the world, Gauteng is a vast experiment. The city region's population continues to expand and diversify, creating a population composed of islands of communities amid seas of strangers. Continued mobility and limited interaction with formal state institutions often leaves people disconnected, oriented to lives well beyond the spaces in which they live. The novelty and social fragmentation of places across the country means formal institutions are often outpaced by the sheer rapidity of change. Many of Gauteng's townships and informal settlements consequently appear ungoverned and remain largely beyond the reach of elected officials and constitutional orders. Yet these are not anarchic spaces. The violence and marginalisation described in these stories may well be the social expression of new political orders. Indeed, as sites of domination and resistance, cities generate new forms of social and political life. A more holistic, human perspective of these new urban spaces reveals forms of non-state, social regulation – family, patriarchy, gangsters, ethnicity – that are far more powerful. The stories in this volume are glimpses into the making of a nation: what it means to be of and in South Africa and a making of membership and belonging in a post-modern, post-colonial era.

FINDING THE WORDS

Estifanos Worku Abeto does not fit the typical 'victim' that the journalist almost instinctively seeks when violence breaks out; his is a story that complicates the migrancy and xenophobia narrative in ways the media often doesn't have the space or time to unravel. We tend to prefer the straightforward angle that helps sort the grey into binaries of black and white, sources that help us pour the complex into soundbites and stories of 500 words or less.

We knew early on that Worku Abeto's story was not a simple one. But it was only after finding him again – following a chance meeting with the African Diaspora Forum where we produced a photograph taken during the 2008 attacks that led us back to him – that we realised just how complicated it was. The destitute person we first met in the refugee camp had been a relatively privileged and educated man who had been a member of the ruling party in Ethiopia, the same party accused of committing atrocious human rights violations over many years. He was also a man on the run because he had finally left his party at a time in which he believed it was the end of its rule, leaving his own life in jeopardy. Here, too, was a deeply religious person in his seventies, a man who had travelled across the continent under dangerous and strenuous conditions, landing in an inhospitable foreign country whose citizens attacked him, beat him and stole what little he had. This was a man living under a government and in an international community that wanted to ignore him at best and, at worst, to send him to his death or to a life in prison. A man who very likely may never see his wife, his children or his country ever again.

Choosing Worku Abeto was an unscientific process and mirrored how we ended up choosing the other narrators for the book. Twelve contributing writers joined us for this collection, each interviewing one narrator and helping to craft their stories, initially drafting brief descriptions of those they chose to write about. To create the stories, we undertook an open-ended process designed to generate unexpected encounters and awkward, uncomfortable questions. We chose narrators who were most likely to 'rub against the grain', to speak of experiences associated with migration, displacement, xenophobia and xenophobic violence that would be both revealing and unsettling. We excluded those who had clear political agendas, who would shape stories following familiar tropes and predictable plotlines. The conversations occurred in a variety of languages and at locations across Gauteng province over almost a year. Where translation into English was required, this was done exclusively by the writers.

Dudu Ndlovu, a Zimbabwean, initially interviewed the self-professed anti-foreigner activist Lufuno Gogoro in 2012 for a research project around xenophobia and social cohesion, returning to him in curiosity: what made this outspoken and dedicated community leader tick? Oupa Nkosi met Lucas Machel when he was reporting on Operation Fiela for the *Mail & Guardian*; he was drawn to the Mozambican bricklayer who was determined to make something of himself in this foreign place. Eliot Moleba, a playwright, roamed the streets of Snake Park until he found the family home of Siphiwe Mahori, the murdered boy he had only read about in the news. When Moleba finally found the house, he found Mahori's mother, Nombuyiselo Ntlane, in her front yard, washing a carpet.

'It was midday and I had been searching for her the whole morning,' says Moleba. 'After we exchanged brief greetings I explained to her who I was and why I had sought to find her. She told me a horrifying story about "people like me" who came to visit her family, making all sorts of promises to get their story and then disappear without a trace. She recalled how one journalist promised that they were going to write to the president so that the day their child was killed could be turned into a holiday, something like a modern-day Hector Pieterson. It was clear that their experience with media in general had not been a good one and they wanted to stay away from it. Yet, perhaps my willingness to hear these stories and search for her served to temporarily exclude me from "people like that".'

Ntlane experienced the disappearing act that even the most well-intentioned journalists and researchers are familiar with: take down the story, leave the scene. But it is the systemic media failures that allowed a 14-year-old boy's killing to disappear from the headlines – more than the empty promises of a misguided reporter – that makes the ethical miscarriage perhaps even more insidious.

While this series of very personal tellings attempts to address some of the shortcomings of journalistic and academic writing – too little space, too little time, too few of the voices of the people, not enough follow-up or follow-through – oral history is not without flaw. Even the process of the interview comes with its own complications. Who is taking the story down? Where is the story being recorded? Is it in the person's home? In their workplace? Who else is present as the interview takes place? And, in this instance of discussions around migrancy, foreignness and deep-rooted xenophobia, which writer is taking the story from which narrator? Are they the same or different nationalities? Different ethnic groups? Races? Genders? In whose language are they speaking? Are they from different economic classes? Do they have similar educations? How might these things change the narrator's willingness to speak openly? What is being withheld? What is being told for the benefit of the interviewer? What is at stake?

From the start, we admitted this and embraced the art of combined efforts. Those taking down and writing the stories – as well as the narrators who told them – were a jumble of people from different countries, of different ages, different genders. They spoke numerous languages, were from various socio-economic classes and came with assorted academic and professional backgrounds. In the end, it was a jumble that reflects contemporary urban South Africa in many ways, but in one particularly important way. This text is distinct in that it speaks so explicitly and intentionally across and about our divides.

Nkosi, an experienced South African journalist, was ashamed when Machel, a Mozambican, admitted he felt unsafe around South Africans – something Machel revealed only after hours of interviews. At the same time, Nkosi is acutely aware of what is driving his fellow South Africans to sometimes act in disturbing and desperate ways.

'Hearing how Lucas feels made me worry that what has happened in his country and other African countries might come to haunt us,' says Nkosi. 'Our economy is now unstable and more and more people are finding it hard to survive. This bubble of frustration and anxiety keeps on increasing each day and eventually it's going to blow. Sharing limited resources and land, which the government is failing to address, has brought fear into black communities. More are willing to fight and even if it means they have to kill, they will. Corruption has added more frustration. Sadly, these fights are between black people against other black people while the minority population still lives in harmony with many resources in their pockets.'

Meanwhile, Tanya Zack, who has written extensively about the inner city, actively sought a narrator who was white – someone she would be able to relate to readily, and, more importantly, she felt would relate more easily to her.

'I had grown up in the inner city of Joburg and Alberton, and there was something about Harry and his history in Yeoville and Hillbrow and the inner city and walking those streets that appealed to me,' she says of Koulaxizis. 'There is a disarming honesty about him, a Joburg mixture of anger and bitterness directed at the system and the state and hopefulness, promise and optimism, a sense of huge opportunity. His own language is racist, yet tolerant and inclusionary. I only found out in the fourth interview that he was married to an Indian woman, and it only came out when he wondered aloud, "Where must I go?" He could have said from the start, "Listen, man, I'm not a racist, I'm married to an Indian woman," which is such a South African thing to say – that you are not racist because you are somehow involved with black people. But he doesn't trade on it in that way. It's this race thing with South Africans that speaks with forked tongue all the time.'

This is the sort of complexity that these pieces, each in their own way, scratched away at, that sense of otherness that sits within all of us – foreign or South African, narrator or transcriber – and that Zack found in Koulaxizis' rooted rootlessness.

'He really is part and parcel of that environment and yet so thoroughly displaced,' Zack says. 'That does something different to the usual otherness, that insider/outsider take. He wasn't an outsider. He was a white guy but wasn't an outsider in that environment. It just makes it all more blurred.'

Collectively, the stories became, not merely a series of voices about migrancy or xenophobia, but something larger that dug more deeply at what it means to be in South Africa today – at what it means to make a nation. It is also what Caroline Wanjiku Kihato, a Kenyan-born researcher and writer interested in migrancy and cities, found in Papi Thetele's own individual story.

'It became a story about contemporary South Africa, and how different groups are struggling to just make a life, and Papi almost epitomises it,' says Kihato. 'The story was about the politics of the township, and the history of South Africa and apartheid segregation. He grew up as an activist, participated in the youth uprising in 1976, was around for the Sharpeville Massacre. And then the country awakened to a new democracy where he had no role anymore. And now he is trying to find a place in the new South Africa for himself.'

While Kihato called the process of taking Thetele's story down and crafting it into a narrative in his own words as a 'co-production', Moleba said he found himself a 'curator' of Ntlane's words.

'The narrator had an unusual power in the writing process because it was their story and their words,' he says of the process of crafting Ntlane's narrative. 'I could only say what she said in the words she used to say it. My role was to be true to her words, and it was a gratifying experience to let someone own their story.'

It was this sort of nuanced understanding which those of us involved in the project hoped to reveal. We wanted to build on the kind of in-depth interviews that often remain confined to academic research reports and papers, artefacts rarely read beyond the academy. The next block of the build was to take the raw words and transform the narrator into their own storyteller.

These pages contain the narrators' words, but these are not interview transcripts, nor were they intended to be. Some of the narrators are gifted storytellers whose accounts required little intervention. Other accounts are mosaics, pieced together from multiple fragments to tell a compelling story. The final results were shared with the narrators and discussed; all were approved by them for publication. Where requested by narrators, we have altered the names of people and places.

We set out to understand what was driving South Africans to turn on those unlike themselves in these explosive xenophobic attacks, but sometimes what we came away with was the more mundane, the stuff of everyday life. As Eggers suggests in *The Voice of Witness Reader*, humans are so much more than their trauma. Their histories cannot be placed into binaries, their experiences do not cross at neat angles. These are the things that linger, these are the stories that do not disappear.

LOREN B LANDAU AND TANYA PAMPALONE

1

A BED OF HIS OWN BLOOD

Nombuyiselo Ntlane

AGE WHEN INTERVIEWED: 42
BORN: Block 4, Snake Park, Soweto, Johannesburg, South Africa
INTERVIEWED IN: Block 8, Snake Park, Soweto, Johannesburg, South Africa
INTERVIEWED BY: Eliot Moleba
PHOTOGRAPHED BY: Oupa Nkosi

Nombuyiselo Ntlane is the mother of Siphiwe Mahori, a 14-year-old who was shot dead on 19 January 2015 by Sheik Yusuf, a Somalian shopkeeper in Soweto. The murder triggered a wave of lootings and xenophobic attacks that made national headlines, attracting the attention of prominent political figures such as Winnie Mandela, who visited the family in the aftermath. Ntlane lives with her husband Daniel Mahori, their two children, a cousin and three grandchildren in a small three-roomed house. Ntlane and Mahori live in one bedroom, their oldest son lives in the other bedroom and the rest of the children share a big couch in the area that serves as a living room and kitchen. Both are unemployed and survive by renting three one-roomed shacks in their backyard to a South African family and two Mozambican families; 14 people live in the yard, which is the size of the 18-yard box of a football pitch.

I'm a mother of four children. I gave birth to my first son on 25 June 2000. When he arrived, we named him Siphiwe, which means 'gift', because his father had always wanted a son. This is why he saw him as our gift from the Lord. As part of the gift, we were happy that our son belonged to the born-free generation. Unlike when we were born, this was a good time to bring life into this world because black people were free and no longer living under apartheid. We were no longer going to be called kaffirs, we were no longer going to be called names.

Before this, if a baas called you something, you were afraid to say anything back but now things are different. We have the right to speak our mind. You can go wherever you want, anytime you want. It is our time to be free. And we wanted our Siphiwe to enjoy the opportunities of our freedom.

Growing up, Siphiwe didn't like to talk much. He was quiet like his father. He loved bicycles, especially fixing them. He loved working with his hands. He had faith in his hands because he could do everything for himself. Even in school, he was interested in learning about building construction and electric wiring.

At the end of the year he asked me to buy him bricks and cement so that he could show me what he was learning at school. I had only bought the cement and was going to buy bricks but it ended just like that; he didn't show me what his life was holding for him. He wanted to build a wall to make our front fence. He promised us that he would build that wall. He was telling me that when he was looking at this house, that it was not built properly.

'How do you know, my child?' I would ask.

He would say, 'This house was not built properly because when you build it's not supposed to be two fingers like this. You see, if you can fit two fingers like this [measuring the cement between the bricks] you know it's not done properly. Look at other places, you can't even fit one finger. I will show you when I build my own house how a house is built because in school we are taught that when you build like this, you are doing it correctly and when you are doing it like this, you are doing it wrong.'

I could see that the work he did in school was really good. I always told him it was good that he knew what is right and what is wrong. Now the children he used to fix bicycles for miss him because the person they used to hang out with, someone they used to laugh with, is no longer here. Even when his father fixed the car, he would help him because he wanted to know how to do it himself so that he doesn't struggle tomorrow. I guess you can say he was a mechanic.

But there was an evil force out there who could see that tomorrow this child could be wealthy so it is better to remove him. And then it removed him. But we say it's okay. It is only the Lord who knows.

I SENT HIM TO BUY A COLD DRINK, NOT TO DIE

On that day I had sent him, I had sent him to the *spaza* shop to buy a cold drink. It was in the evening of 19 January 2015; I think it was after 7 pm. My husband and I were watching a soccer game. I remember that the children were sleeping because they had just returned from playing outside, so they were exhausted. We wanted to drink some Coke, so we called Siphiwe who was still playing soccer outside on the street with his friends. When we called him, he came running. That's the kind of son he was. We had taught him to always listen to his elders. He was very cheerful when he left the house. And then after that, after a short while, around ten minutes later, I heard a child screaming at the gate:

'*Mme wa Siphiwe! Mme wa Siphiwe!* Siphiwe is shot!'

'*Hao,* Siphiwe is shot? Where did they shoot him?' I asked.

'The shop at the top!' they said.

We still didn't know what had happened when my husband and I rushed to see him. We didn't even know if there was hope that Siphiwe was going to survive because we live at a distance from the shop, and it must have taken a long time for the children to run to the house to call us and then run back with us.

When we finally arrived, at first we couldn't see him because there was a big crowd of people around him. Many people were just looking in. I think no one really understood what they were supposed to do to save his life.

We found him sleeping on a bed of his own blood. Some people called the ambulance and they said it was on the way. We also called the ambulance and they said it would be on the way. In the meantime, we tried to protect him, to close the bullet wound with something. We used this red jersey I'm wearing; his father pressed it against the wound to close it or slow down the bleeding. We wanted to protect his blood. He was bleeding too much, losing too much blood.

You see, the way the blood was coming out so fast, it was coming out like it was being pumped out. It was gushing out. And we tried to close it but it was already too late. The jersey was drenched and soaking wet with blood; it was more red. And we still tried and tried and tried. We called the ambulance again. We called many, many times. We phoned and phoned and phoned and they just said we are coming – but over 20 minutes later, we were still waiting for them. And then when we saw the police, we stopped them and asked if they could help us because my child was laying there and now he had lost a lot of blood. And so the police hurried to the police station to bring the ambulance. His father told him that help was coming. You could see that Siphiwe wanted to say something; we could see his lips moving like he was trying to talk but no voice came out. His father held him and told him that he was going to be alright. But while we were waiting for the police to fetch the ambulance, my child had lost a lot of blood … he gave up. It was the end, just like that. So I thought if maybe had we found help in time, my child was supposed to be alive because doctors would have known what to do. But they arrived late.

Today I still can't understand how he was shot at the shop at the top when I sent him to the other shop. I still don't understand. I suspect the reason he was shot there could be because there might have been some kind of a fight at the other shop. There are kids who smoke *nyaope*, and they are often found arguing with *makula*. The *nyaope* boys loot their stores. They take things from their stores and run away, then *makula* chase after them and whenever they catch them that's when they return whatever they took. You know, it must have been something like that.

So when my child left the house he must have seen what was happening there is not right and then maybe he must have decided to go to buy the Coke at the other shop. Maybe the shop owner told himself or thought that my son was another member of the *nyaope* boys who wanted to steal from the shop.

In the past, there were also lootings and xenophobic attacks that took place in other parts of Johannesburg, and maybe he thought they were beginning to spread to Snake Park. Perhaps the shop owner thought that he was under some kind of an attack by the people outside. But my son wasn't the person who came with those things, he was just a person who came to buy a cold drink. In fact, he was in front of the entrance so it should have been obvious that he was a person who came to buy. But the shop owner shot a bullet through the door and then it happened that my child was the one who was hit … I sent him to buy a cold drink, not to die.

And then my child lost his life just like that. We lost our gift.

DENIED OUR DAY IN COURT

The investigating officer who handled our case told us to wait for the court updates from him. He said he would let us know when the court proceedings began. But he never contacted us, so we never really knew what was happening.

As far as we have heard from other people, Sheik Yusuf stayed in police custody until his bail application was heard early in February 2015 at the Protea Magistrate's Court. The police officer didn't tell us about the bail hearing, so we couldn't attend it. We were told Yusuf defended himself by saying that my child was there to rob them. I even read somewhere that he said the gun they used to shoot my son was a gun that he brought with him. I don't know if Siphiwe even knew how to hold a gun. They said that he dropped it in their shop and then they took it and shot him with it. I think he was saying this to protect himself so that the judge could see him as a

victim and be lenient. And maybe that's why Yusuf was granted bail of R2 000 for his freedom. R2 000? That is the price of freedom. But what about the life of my child? How can they grant him bail? He killed a young child who still had a lot of time ahead of him, a time to be a child and grow up to discover what he wants to do with his life or learn what life holds for him out there.

My son was a child. It was not even like you could say that person was a thief, he was a child of 14 years. I don't think that you, as you are, can be mugged by a child of 14 years.

I was hurt a lot by the court.

To make matters worse, during the court proceedings, while we were heartbroken by what this man did to us and our child, the court didn't ask to hear from us, as parents of the child. They didn't call us, which means everything that was said by the shop owner, whether true or not, to them it was right. They should have called us, as parents of the child, and asked us questions to verify that when this person says this and that, is it true? But they failed to call us to ask. They denied us our day in court so that we can also speak for ourselves and our son. I think they believed everything the shop owner told them to be the truth.

For example, I don't deny that before the funeral, the elders of the shop owner came to the house and they asked for forgiveness. They accepted that what their relative did was wrong. They didn't like it either, as business owners. So they left some money. It was R15 000. When they got to court, they said it was R30 000, which was a lie.

You see, when it came to things like these we should have at the very least been called to the court to tell our side of the story. They needed to ask us directly whether this person had really left that much money or not. But they failed to ask us. Everything that came from him was right, including his lies. In the end, they set him free.

And wherever Yusuf is, I don't know how he feels, I don't know if he feels proud of what he did to Siphiwe, to kill a child, a 14-year-old boy and then say it was *nyaope* when my child did not smoke *nyaope*. Or even cigarettes, he didn't smoke them. He was still a child. He listened to everything I said to him because he knew he was still a child. When I said, 'Siphiwe, this is wrong,' he knew it. And when I said, 'Siphiwe, this is right,' he knew it too. He was a child who, if you could see him, you would see that this is a child who was well behaved. He was everyone's child in our street. If you sent him somewhere, he would run and return with the message.

It is painful what happened to us and my son.

The family were so far removed from the court proceedings that when asked what the verdict of the case was, Ntlane couldn't answer. All she read or heard about the case was from news reports that said Sheik Yusuf was a free man.

WE WILL NOT ASK FOR HIS HEAD

One of the earliest memories of being happy as a child is my mother's love. She was a kind and quiet person who didn't like to talk much.

But she was also very strict with my siblings. I grew up with my brother and sister. I was the middle child. Despite her strictness, we were always happy because our mother gave us love all the time. As a parent, she shared her happiness with us. Like God who loved his children equally, my mother didn't have favourites. She was also a special woman who took us to church every Sunday. Every Sunday, no matter what was happening, we always had to go to church. I grew up in a house of prayer. This made God the centre of our lives.

Today my favourite days are Thursday and Sunday. On Thursdays I attend women's prayer day at church. I love it because all the women in church get together for a Bible study. We all read the Bible and discuss issues of our faith as women and mothers. I enjoy the support I get from the group a lot. On Sundays I wake up, cook, clean up and bath the kids and then take them to church. This is the day that makes me happy because we get to sing, dance and worship together as a family. We always enjoy ourselves. And when you are enjoying yourself you don't think about the sad things. It's good to forget them for a while. God brings us comfort. That's what my family always finds at church.

At the moment I'm just getting used to the loss and pain. I just tell myself that it's okay. It's okay. Life has to move on, but when I see a picture of him … that feeling … even when you are just looking at his clothes … you know, that feeling comes to you, of how I used to hold him. So I tell myself to let it pass. During this time the Bible helps me a great deal. Right now, one of the verses that comforts me enormously is found in the book of Deuteronomy, chapter 28, verses 1 and 7:

> Now it shall come to pass, if you diligently obey the voice of the Lord your God, to observe carefully all His commandments which I command you today, that the Lord your God will set you high above all nations of the earth. And all these blessings shall come upon you and overtake you, because you obey the voice of the Lord your God. The Lord will cause your enemies who rise

against you to be defeated before your face; they shall come out against you one way and flee before you seven ways.

When my child was killed, this is one of the verses that blessed me. You know, when you listen to it, it tells you that if someone does something bad to you, don't respond by doing something bad to them. Speak to God, he will deal with them for you.

That's why when the shop owner was arrested and then immediately released on bail, I didn't say let's look for him and find him wherever he was and do bad things to him. Even our community was angry and wanted to find him so they can teach him a lesson. In fact, our community said that they must all leave after my son was killed because they don't know how to live with us. But weeks and months after they didn't leave, some people wanted to chase all the foreign-owned *spaza* shops out. We told them not to use our son's death as an excuse to loot or attack other shop owners.

I think the community was angry because everyone could see that it was unfair that he was not convicted even when it was obvious that he had killed someone. But we had to make peace with the decision of the court. When the court released him, I turned to God and said God is the one who knows everything, he knows what will happen. In fact, he is the one who will judge us all. And I left it there. I spoke with my husband. I said, 'No, let's leave it. God is there and He will answer for us.'

Today there are new Somalians running the *spaza* shop where my son was killed. I don't like it and some people also don't like it. But we all still buy from them. I don't feel good about it but I just told myself that we will learn to live with it. This is how my family and I are dealing with the situation. We will not avenge or ask for his head. But who knows what will happen to Sheik Yusuf. It could be something worse than what he did to our child.

Postscript: Following the shooting, Sheik Yusuf was taken into police custody and, according to court transcripts, he was charged with culpable homicide, possession of an unlicensed firearm and discharging the firearm in a public area. Weeks later, the 33-year-old was granted bail of R2 000. Yusuf told the judge that a mob outside of his shop was trying to break in and he shot to defend himself. No witnesses were called, despite one witness having been mentioned during the proceedings as shot during the incident and in hospital. In the court transcripts, the family was not mentioned once in any of the official proceedings. In September 2015, Yusuf pleaded guilty to all charges. The judge ruled to wholly suspend the sentence for culpable homicide and possession of an unlicensed firearm, and dismissed outright the charges of possession and discharging a firearm in a public area. Sheik Yusuf served no jail time. The shooting incident which led to Siphiwe's death made national headlines, hurling the country into another wave of xenophobic violence. But the final ruling on the case received virtually no media coverage.

2

THIS COUNTRY IS MY HOME

Azam Khan

AGE WHEN INTERVIEWED: **36**
BORN: **Punjab, Pakistan**
INTERVIEWED IN: **Rosslyn, Pretoria, South Africa**
INTERVIEWED BY: **Nedson Pophiwa**
PHOTOGRAPHED BY: **Madelene Cronje**

Azam Khan is one of the many hawkers trading in Rosslyn, an industrial area in Pretoria North, where he repairs cellphones and sells cellphone accessories. He has lived in South Africa since 1999. Whereas many of his fellow Pakistanis tend to distance themselves from the local communities, focused on living to work so they can return home with money saved, Khan has learnt to speak Setswana, one of the 11 official languages of South Africa, and married a Tswana woman. He says he has lived for too long in South Africa to still call himself a foreigner.

Looking back in time, I cannot understand how I really ended up living here in South Africa. Maybe if I had stayed in Pakistan things would have been different for me. I would've been working there for government, maybe, and staying close to my family. But because I wasn't doing anything meaningful after school I had to find something to do.

My dream was to work as a soldier or a policeman or any other government job. I was a good sportsman back in high school, playing cricket and basketball, which means I wouldn't have struggled doing any of those jobs. I even had a bursary to complete my matric at the school where I was, simply because I was good in sports.

Our family was made up of my father, mother, three sisters and a brother in Punjab. Our parents could do anything to make us happy. My father died when I was about 16 so my mother was responsible for raising us after that. I can't say we were suffering, as such, because we never went to bed hungry. But you know a lot of people in my family, especially the extended family, always found a place to migrate to and live there. Some of them live in England and I have an aunt who lives with her family in the United States. So I was sure maybe one day I would join them.

Growing up I went to a boys' school. When it comes to the schools, Muslims always prefer to have separate schools for boys and girls. I was a good student: my grades were usually high and sometimes I even got a prize in class. You know I can't believe what really happened because I was a good cricketer and a basketballer. I even played the top schools in cricket competitions. I was a good batsman and bowler; let's just say I was an all-rounder in cricket. I could have been playing national cricket, but really I don't know how I ended up not playing in competitions after matric. Basketball – same thing. I loved it and was very good. As you can see with my height, I was tall, even then in high school, so I had an advantage. That could have been my life but, *eish*.

I was a teenager then, you know, just doing nothing with my life after matric, hanging out with my friends, all of us basically not working or being responsible with our lives. I had not even tried to look for a job. You know, as a young man you really don't have a clue about life; you're just immature and waiting for your parents to do everything for you.

But here I am so many years later, selling these cellphone chargers and repairing phones on the pavement of a shop. Those science experiments we did in school helped me at least to understand how to fix electric gadgets so that's what I do now, here. I could have lived in Pakistan working a good job. But I was not mature. I was just a young man after matric who was irresponsible, so I had to grow up and learn from life. But anyway, that is life.

BRIGHT FUTURE

It was 1998, just after matric, and I wasn't working. I stayed at home just hanging out with friends. Then I made friends with a guy who was visiting Pakistan from South Africa, where he was living at the time. He was much older and he told me about his life there. He said it was a place I could start my life and make a bit of money.

There were stories that this country had a bright future, so I thought also that maybe this would be helpful for me. Maybe I would work there or open a business and after some time of making money, I could move back to Punjab. I told my mom that I was going with this guy to South Africa and she was happy for me. The time came and I bid farewell to my family and friends, and set off for Johannesburg in October 1999.

So, I let this friend of mine take me to this place I had never been to. I didn't know much about the country at the time. I also just didn't know a lot as a young man. I assumed there were mostly African people there and a small population of Asians. There was really not much else I had read about the country, but I was pretty sure that all those Pakistani people who went there were making a better living than back home. At the time I arrived I also didn't know how to speak English. I had to learn it when I started living here. The streets taught me English and even Tswana.

BLOWING UP THE MONEY

I remember the day I arrived on the flight from Pakistan with my friend. He took me to my new home in the suburb of Laudium in Pretoria West. I felt at home there because there were other guys from my country who spoke my language and I was quickly introduced to them. I also saw that there were Indian people and some from Bangladesh which made it feel very warm. The first few days I wasn't really bothered to mix with them or to hang out with them because I was just thinking about what my next plan would be in this country.

I had about a thousand dollars with me, which I was supposed to use to start something – maybe a small shop. My mother had helped me with that money and I was looking forward to paying her back. But guess what? My hosts were not very good advisers. They actually helped me to blow up all that money. Within the space of two weeks I blew all that money away in pleasure, having a good time enjoying Pretoria's nightlife. I had never been to any of these clubs with music playing loud, and the girls were just coming to us very easy, you know. I liked it, and partying needs a lot of money, so I just had my fun.

Then I was broke, and I called my mother telling her that I wanted to come back home. I said, 'Mom, I really have to come back. This place is not good for me, I miss home and I think it's best to come back.'

She didn't listen to me or feel sorry for me. She just said – I remember her last words – 'Grow up and stick it out there in South Africa; we don't want you to come back just yet.' So, there I was with such a reply from my mother and I was left with nothing else to do but find a job.

DOOR TO DOOR

My friends in Laudium said they could help me look for something. There were about ten fellow Pakistani guys living in one flat who were working in different jobs around Pretoria as shop assistants, mechanics, technicians and hawkers, and they always shared ideas about how to make money. One of the guys from the flat who worked at the Nazim General Store in downtown Marabastad recruited me to work there as a shop assistant.

The shop was owned by a South African Indian man, and I can't say the owner was a bad guy; I don't remember him shouting at his workers. It was a family business, so his children and wife worked there. It's not always easy when the family members work with you because they also feel like they can give you work to do, like they are all your bosses. You know, as a general store they were selling a variety of goods like groceries, clothes, bicycles, radios, TVs and other lots of different stuff. I couldn't help but study these new surroundings carefully and was thinking of ideas about how to be my own boss. I couldn't stand these instructions from the shop owners; every day I wanted to quit because I was not used to it. I was also learning English in the streets.

While working in the store, I could not help but notice the guys who were passing through our shop who were raking in my monthly salary within a couple days' work. I was getting R200 every week but these guys were making sometimes up to R400 every day. They were selling watches, earrings and some other accessories, you know? I used to see them coming to shops in Marabastad to order stock. I would ask them where they were taking these goods to and they told me that in the townships you can go from house to house selling these things because people like them, sometimes even buying on credit. So I said well, let me quit and start selling watches. This was long before cellphones flooded the market. The thoughts of going back home had died away as I began making money every day. I only worked in the shop for a month and then I quit.

You know after a year, sometime in 2000, I was getting more and more money from the sales. Can you believe? I was even now going to townships in Pretoria like Ga-Rankuwa, Mabopane, Soshanguve, walking door to door, selling in the people's houses. I even went to Mamelodi and in the taxi ranks to sell my stuff. At one time I was also going from Pretoria to Tembisa and getting orders from many of my customers.

A year later I was making a lot more profit and I decided to talk to a shop owner here in Rosslyn and he allowed me to rent a table outside his shop. I put on that table some radios, TVs, shaving machines, locks, cassettes and CDs – you know there were still a few people using them – watches, you know. My customers just bought everything from my table and it was like a real shop to me. Christmas was the best time; I made even double the other months. I bought a car and was having a good life.

One thing about this money I was making is that I was still too young and immature; I was making a lot and spending a lot.

WE DON'T WANT A *MAKULA* HERE

I met my wife on one of my usual door-to-door sales trips in the township – in Ga-Rankuwa in 2001. I knocked on this particular door and an attractive young lady came to the door and opened it. You know, the moment I saw her, I could feel in my heart that I loved her. I didn't hesitate to ask her name, and told her I was going to come and see her again. You know, those days there were no cellphones, but anyway we used to make appointments and then would meet in the streets near her house. She was living with her grandfather, and he did not know about our relationship. I sometimes would come to their house like I was selling watches as a way to see her.

She had just completed her matric and didn't know what she was going to do with her life. She kind of reminded me of those days when I was still home, trying to think of what to do next in my life. But you know what? One day we realised she was pregnant. I said I will marry this woman and so I approached her family. I wasn't sure how to go about the process of lobola but some guys in the township told me that I was expected to pay some money for cows and then buy some gifts for the family. Obviously, this was all new to me but I wanted my girlfriend to be my wife.

There was a terrible incident one day when I was visiting her. An uncle of hers saw us and he was not happy at all. This *malume* was very angry because he was so against the relationship.

Can you see this scar on my hand? It was this uncle who stabbed me. He ended up stabbing me with a knife on my wrist, shouting 'Hey, we don't want a *makula* here; go away!' I had to rush outside and avoid being stabbed some more with that pocket knife.

I remember very well how I was bleeding on the one hand, driving with the other one back to my place in Laudium. I was afraid and also very angry because now I really wanted to marry this woman but her family was being tough on me. I don't think I cared what this man was thinking about me or if he was going to accept me, because what mattered to me was my woman and the family we wanted to start. I just said I will keep my distance from her family if they don't want to see me.

But that was the only incident when I was shown negative feelings by the family members. Maybe they thought I was trying to use their daughter by marrying her, but I was just in love. Slowly, slowly they accepted me as a son-in-law. So later, in 2002, I approached her family to pay lobola. We talked about it and I negotiated for R8 000, paid all of it and we were now officially married.

Now my wife and I have three children. All of them are girls. The oldest one is almost 15, followed by a nine-year-old, and the youngest is seven. With my assistance, financially, my wife enrolled in a nursing school, which became her job even up to now.

We have now been married for so many years. That *malume*, I still see him every time I see the family and now we have become very good friends. We joke about that incident because it was a long time ago.

But I was never really a victim of xenophobic violence like those other cases you read about in the news. I just experience things on a daily basis; attitudes like people calling me *makula*. It doesn't bother me; I just hustle.

LOSING EVERYTHING

As the years went past, my business continued to grow. After some time, I told the owner of the shop where I was renting the table that I now wanted to expand my business. So we agreed that I would rent a shop from him where I now sold electronic gadgets.

God was helping me. Business was good. I was driving a Nissan Sentra at that time and it looked fancy. I was feeling good about life and my achievements. I was also having fun with friends, drinking, partying and hanging out with girls sometimes.

It was a friend who introduced me to the casino one day. I had never visited one before in my life. Imagine – on the first night I won about R5 000! I said to myself that standing for long hours at my shop I was not making such good money as one night gambling. This was the beginning of my downfall. After a year, I lost everything; my car and my reliable source of income dried up so fast that I had to ask my wife for help. We left the suburbs of Pretoria North where we were staying and had to go to the township to rebuild our lives. This was a very low moment in my life; I felt very sad about it – but it happened. I was immature and irresponsible because of gambling.

It was 2005 when I lost my shop. But this was not the only thing I had to deal with. At the time I was making good money and I was able to buy stock from wholesalers on credit. I think at that time I was owing almost R45 000 to the people that were supplying me. My wife was not working at the time and we had a family to support. I had to sell my shop to someone else, but the money was too little.

These people wanted their money and I was scared they were gonna kill me or do something bad to my family. I phoned a friend of mine and decided to live with him in Burgersfort, there in Limpopo. I was trying to lay low a bit but the problem is that we didn't have any money to keep staying there. My friend also didn't have enough money to take care of us or to lend me so that I could start my life again. He actually wanted me to work for him but he couldn't pay me for the services. I was really in a bad situation at the time. I still tried to phone my friends in Pretoria so that they could help me out, but no one was willing.

Guess who came to my rescue? My unemployed wife. She contacted the people I was owing money to and they told her how much the money was. She talked to them nicely so that they would give me a chance to pay it all back and after three months I came back to Pretoria to meet those guys and we agreed I could pay every month until I settled the debt.

Man, it was not easy. I went to friends again, but no one was willing to lend me money, even the ones I was spending the money with; they just didn't want to give me a little something to start again. It was rough. They even reminded me of those days I was doing the gambling.

My wife's grandfather gave me R300 from his pension grant so that I could buy some stock. So I went to Laudium where I used to get stock and bought some, then I was back on the streets selling in houses of the townships. Every little cent I was making was going back to those guys and paying what I was owing them. It was tough because I could leave the house at 6 am and catch a train to town and start selling my watches and sometimes arrived back to the house only after 9 pm. The whole day I was just on the streets, trying to get back on my feet.

My wife's family was so good to me, you know? Especially that grandfather, he was a nice old man. He liked me so much and believed in me. He died about seven years ago and left us that house where we are now living.

The debt was paid after about two years and I continued with my business. But now also my wife got a job as a nurse at the local clinic and I am embarrassed to say ever since then I have become relaxed. I don't work as hard as before. The car I own now is not as nice as the one I had before. But what can I do? It's all I can afford. I really feel like I will never get back to those days of my own shop. I still want to have another one like it, but I have no money to go big again with my business plans.

BACK IN PUNJAB

I have not been to Pakistan since coming to South Africa but I speak to my mother and my sisters whenever I can. We have a good relationship and they miss me too much.

Years ago, when I got married, I told my mother, and she has no problem with me being married here. I even sent her pictures of my wife and children. They always ask when they will see them. But even if they didn't approve of my marriage there's nothing they can really do about it. It's my life. Whenever I have money I send some to my mother and sisters so that they can buy things they want. When my life was going fine I used to send them a lot of money, but now I can send maybe just once in a year and it's not the same amount of money like before.

They keep asking me when I am coming home to visit them. But I have no money. I need about R8 000 for the flight then a lot more to spend when I go there, because I can't just arrive empty-handed. If it was those years when business was booming I would have easily afforded to visit home. Maybe this December I will go there. But to be honest, another part of my heart tells me that South Africa is home to me. These three children were born here and because of my wife I cannot imagine starting life again in Pakistan. If only I can bounce back in business, I will be happy.

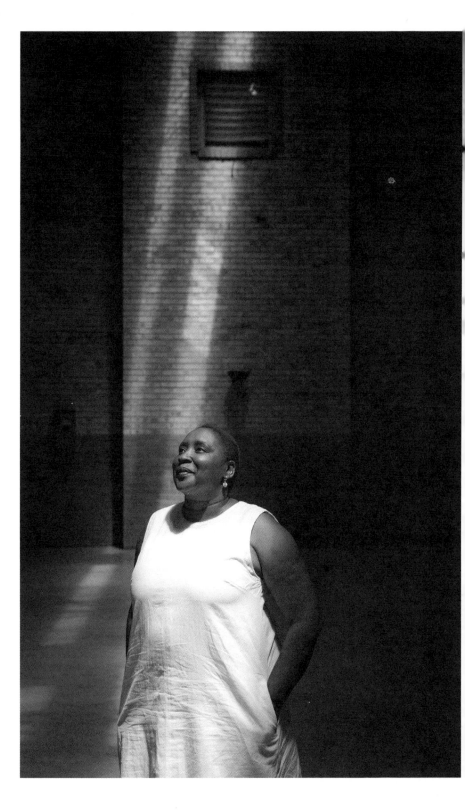

3

ON PATROL IN THE DARK CITY

Ntombi Theys

AGE WHEN INTERVIEWED: **48**
BORN: Alexandra, Johannesburg, South Africa
INTERVIEWED IN: Alexandra, Johannesburg, South Africa
INTERVIEWED BY: Ryan Lenora Brown
PHOTOGRAPHED BY: Madelene Cronje

Ntombi Theys is a lifelong resident of Alexandra, one of Johannesburg's oldest black townships. Her childhood sprawled across one of the most violent times in the neighbourhood's history, as it became an epicentre of protest and resistance against the apartheid regime. For much of her adult life, Theys has been deeply involved in city politics as a ward committee member and community organiser, working to reduce the neighbourhood's high rates of poverty and unemployment, and to fight crime in the area. She told her story at the offices of the Alexandra Stadium, where she works as an administrator, and at her home in Alexandra.

You know those black, black winter nights, the kind when you put your hand out and can't even see your fingers? That's how it was. Very dark and very cold. I'd been calling the city for months complaining about the streetlight outside. People could fall, I told them. People could be robbed. It's not safe for a street to not have light, I said. But in actual fact, things can take a long time to get fixed in Alex, things can take a long time to change, and so that night the light was still off.

My little house is attached to my mother's, and she has the tub, so when I woke up, around 5 am, I went around to her side to bath there. Only when I got close, that's when I could see something was really wrong.

Her door was open and the bars on the window were all twisted up. When I looked in, it was like the place was full of holes. A hole where the TV was supposed to be. A hole where the heater was supposed to be. The microwave was gone; so was the kettle. They'd even dragged our fridge halfway from the kitchen to the front door, but I guess that one was too much, or maybe they got spooked, because they left it right there next to the couch.

At first, I was afraid to go any further. My mother and my daughter were inside, *neh*? And it wouldn't be the first time you hear of someone being shot and killed for a television in Alex. In actual fact, that's how it often is.

But I made myself do it and thank God, they were alive and asleep on the bed. They'd slept through the whole thing. The guys even took their cellphones from the bed beside them and they didn't wake up once. Thank God, I kept saying. Thank God.

Once we'd all had a look around, I went to the police station. It was maybe 6 am then, just starting to get light. Two cops came back with me to the house and started asking me questions: 'Is there anyone you suspect? Did you hear anything? What's missing?' They wrote all the answers in a tiny notebook, then one of them started dusting for fingerprints. He dusted on the door they broke through, and on the fridge, and around the countertop. Then they were gone.

Those cops never came back. When I called about the fingerprints, they said, 'We didn't get any hits. We can't find them.' They didn't sound surprised at all. So then I said, 'How come you can't find them?' And they just said, 'These people whose fingerprints we took: they're not in our system.'

Now why would someone not be in the system? There's only one reason I know. They're foreign. They don't have an ID. Those guys come here to do crime because they know our police can't find them. They know they can get away with it. I've seen it happen so many times, and it's always the same story.

OLD ALEX

When the businessman Stephen Papenfus bought a large tract of farmland north of Johannesburg in 1904, he originally hoped to turn it into a white neighbourhood. But when prospective buyers complained that it was too far from the city centre, he began selling to black families instead. A decade later, in 1913, the government passed the Natives Land Act, severely restricting where black people could buy and own land, and leaving Alex one of the few freehold black settlements in the city.

My family is old Alex. We have been here from the start, from the time when it was just farms and there was no city up here at all. That was back in the 1920s and my grandfather was working as a farmhand in this area when he caught word that someone was selling plots of land nearby. He was just an ordinary gardener in those days, looking after the crops and the cows and what have you.

But land wasn't so expensive then as it is now, and he was able to save enough to buy himself a little plot. And once you have land, so many things become easier. My grandparents built a house on that land, and then some rooms outside it that they rented out. In actual fact, this land thing made them business people. So that's how it started for my family. We've been here ever since.

In all the time I've known it, Alex has been a mixed-up kind of place. For a long time, before the apartheid government got to us, we had all kinds of people living here – there were Chinese married to coloureds, coloureds married to blacks, blacks married to Indians. My own mother is a Khoisan lady from the Northern Cape. She'd come to Johannesburg after she finished school to look for work, and she was staying with her sister on 14th Avenue.

She met my father at a garage in Orange Grove and they married young, young, young – maybe 18. That's just how it was in those days. His mother didn't approve, really. She probably wanted an African lady, a Xhosa like them, not some coloured girl from Northern Cape. But what could she do? That was Alex. You met everyone here. That was just how life was.

I was the first child, born in 1968, and then after me came four boys. Four! My mother hoped and hoped for another girl, but I was it. We stayed in the yard outside my grandparents' house – all seven of us in one little room that was our bedroom, kitchen, sitting room, dining room, everything all at once. To get to the toilet, you had to walk outside. At night, especially in winter, you just prayed you wouldn't need to go.

Still, I was a child then, hey, so most of the memories I have are good. They called Alex 'the dark city' in those days because we didn't have electricity, but there was something homey even about that. Your mother would keep the house warm in winter by cooking something on the stove, so that the whole place stayed cozy and nice all night. And we used to say back then that we all knew each other even in the dark. We could identify our neighbours by their walk or their shape or their voice. You used to know, even before you got close, that this was Ma Moloi, this was Ma Dlamini, this was Ma Ntuli. There were trees all around – fruit trees – and as kids we used to go up and down picking figs and apricots. Sometimes when we were good, our mother gave us money to go to the shop down the road and buy the thing we called *atchar* bread – *atchar* and polony on a thick piece of white bread – or else peanut-butter sandwiches. That was our menu, and we loved it. You know, Alexandra was so nice then.

So we kids, we were happy, but for my parents, things were getting tough. In 1974, the city council came to us and said, we are buying your house. They didn't ask us, they told. Your choices were either you forfeited the land and took nothing, or you kept the small money they felt like paying you and then became a tenant in your own home. So that's what we did. My grandmother started paying rent on a house she'd owned for 50 years. Like it or not. That was life in Alex too.

And around that time also, my parents' marriage was breaking up. When they first got together, my father was this very proud father. He'd get up early every morning to wash my nappies. He was so excited to have me, his first child. But by the time I was a little older, that was changing. They were fighting a lot and he was cheating and becoming abusive. He would say things like, 'My family have property here, you're nothing without us. You don't even have a family in Alexandra.' And he would hit her. He hit her so much sometimes that she went to sleep outside in the toilets. Finally, she had enough, and she took us kids and she left for the other side of Alex. She worked then in one of the first shoe stores in the new Sandton City mall, so she could be independent from him. She was a tough, tough lady.

LIKE A PIECE OF PAPER TEARING IN HALF

On 16 June 1976, South African police brutally put down a peaceful protest by high-school students in the township of Soweto, south of Johannesburg, killing hundreds. News of the brutality circled the globe, and in the days that followed, the protests rippled outward to other communities nearby. On 18 June, students in Alexandra began a solidarity march with the Soweto students, prompting violent reprisal from the police.

I was still very young then. We saw the protests starting from the windows of our school. We were so afraid. At some point, the teachers told us they wanted to attack our school and we must get

out and run home as quickly as we could. But when we got into the street there were people everywhere and police were shooting and teargassing, so there was no time to go home. I knew an auntie who stayed nearby, so I ran to her place and the two of us hid under her bed. I don't know how long we were there, but eventually my mother showed up to take me home. She was so shaken. On the way there, she watched a woman get shot while she was out buying a tin of milk, a young mother from down our street. 'That AK-47 ripped her skin open like a piece of paper tearing in half,' she told me later. I can't forget that.

Outside it was still hectic, but my mother wanted to get me home, so she grabbed my hand and we went. On the way, we saw the Chinese man who had a shop in front of the school, selling snacks to the kids and all that. He used to always yell after us, 'Schoolboys, schoolboys, come back here,' so that's what we called him too – Schoolboy. For as long as I can remember, he was there in Alex. Well that day people around could see that Schoolboy's life was in danger. He wasn't white, but he was close, *neh*? That could be trouble. So some guys had smeared his face with black shoe polish and then stuck a balaclava over him. They were holding him as if he were drunk, walking him away from the township as quickly as possible like he was a sick uncle they had to get home. In actual fact, they saved his life. We never saw him anymore after that.

WE AREN'T GOING ANYWHERE

Over the course of its history, the city tried repeatedly to uproot and relocate Alexandra residents from their plots on prime land – usually with little success. In the 1960s, they tried a different tack: to turn Alex into a 'hostel city' where workers could be housed in boxy, single-sex dormitories. All family houses would be eliminated. In the late 1970s, a local Dutch Reformed Church reverend, Sam Buti, started the 'Save Alex' campaign to fight forced removals to Soweto and Tembisa.

That was my first time becoming an activist. My mother was very involved in the campaign and she brought me along as well. We wore these white T-shirts that said SAVE ALEXANDRA across the front, and we would go with the reverend to different houses where people were being removed, where their stuff had been put out on the streets. Sometimes they even took their doors and windows off, just to make sure they'd really go. So we went to those houses and we brought it all back in. When they put us out, we put ourselves back in. That was how we did it.

I look back on those days as the beginning of my time organising for the community. I still remember the day we found out we'd won, that the city wouldn't be moving anyone anymore. It was the most exciting day of my life. Just imagine – we were all in the street, screaming, crying, singing, singing, singing until midnight and beyond. 'Our Alex has been saved by God,' people were saying. 'We aren't going anywhere. We're going to stay.'

A few years later, in 1987, I finished school and went to work. By that time, my brother, who had been a student activist, had been arrested and tortured. It turned him somehow. He's never recovered.

Anyway, that same year, I fell pregnant. I was so embarrassed – I was so young! It was supposed to be different for me. But luckily for me the baby's father was 100 per cent involved. We named our daughter Dimakatso – Maki for short – it means 'surprise'. He was a taxi driver; he ran the first taxi business in Alex. And he loved us and cared for us every second of his life, until 28 July 2001, when he was shot seven times in a taxi shootout.

I can remember a few years after Maki was born, how Alex was starting to change. Now, Alex has always been a very diverse place. Those Chinese I mentioned, they were always living with us, talking in Zulu and Sotho and Afrikaans, and we loved them so much. And there were Indians and coloureds like my mother and all of that. We valued that diversity. There were even a few from foreign countries – these Zimbabweans and Malawians who got work in white people's gardens in Joburg and then came to stay with their girlfriends in Alex. But the number wasn't too much, *neh*? Only a few.

It's after Mandela came out that that started to change. I still remember him coming on TV and telling us that we're not going to have electric fences on our borders anymore. People aren't animals. They shouldn't die like animals trying to make a better life. But *yoh*, once that fence was gone, things got too easy for those people coming over.

And bit by bit after that, they began coming here, to Alex. That's when the influx began, and then it became uncontrollable. Why I say uncontrollable is: Alex, all through my life, has been full of people without jobs, without good shelter, without enough food to eat. And all my life, we've been waiting for a government that understands. When the African National Congress (ANC) came in, we believed we had one, *neh*? But then all these foreigners started coming here and offering to work for less than Alex people would. A construction company would say, 'We can pay you this much to work,' and South Africans would say, 'No, no, it's not a living wage, I can't accept it.' But the foreigners accepted that yes, this is not good, but it's better than the situation in my country so I'll take it. That made us feel like our human rights were meaningless, you know? If the Constitution says a man must be given a dignified wage and then a foreigner comes and says he will do it for less, then what does that right mean at all?

THE GOVERNMENT LETS THEM HAVE THE JOBS AND THE HOUSES WE HAVE BEEN WAITING FOR

It was a few years after that that I decided to get into politics. I'm not sure why then, I guess I just couldn't take it anymore. Everywhere you looked in Alex, you saw that the place and the people weren't being developed. Imagine. People living on the streets. People smoking *nyaope* and stealing to pay for it. People dying from HIV, leaving tiny babies with no families. People being burgled by foreign gangs. And you know, if you look at the history of Alex – so many of our best-known politicians got their start here. And yet, this place is not at all developed; it's not at all what it's supposed to be. So I started organising for the ANC, because I thought these are the people who can make this better for people, but only if we make them to do it.

But we were still having so many problems with the crime. And when my own place got burgled in 2013, that was a real wake-up call for me. It wasn't just my house either; so many people on my street were being robbed those days. And the police were always telling them the same thing as they told me – we can't find these guys. They're not in our system. They're foreign. Sometimes someone would even interrupt a robbery and hear those guys speaking a different language – one that doesn't come from South Africa. So that's how we knew it too.

That's when I decided we can't rely on the police anymore to keep us safe. They aren't coming fast enough, and they're not finding these guys. We have to get a community patrol together. I organised all the leaders in my area and we made a plan. We would send out these volunteers in the night, walking door to door and keeping an eye out for these criminals. And then some of us stayed up at night and made them soup and toast and tea and kept an eye on them. Sometimes they'd come across the guys and chase them away. Sometimes they'd shoot at them; whatever they had to do.

But after some months, we had to stop those patrols. We just didn't have the money anymore. That's when I really started to feel so frustrated about what was happening here. These guys were coming here to do crime, *neh*, because they couldn't get what they wanted from their own governments. But in actual fact, our government has to first look to its own citizens. Do you get my point? And we are still such a young democracy.

Our people are frustrated because there was this better life they were promised and instead the government keeps letting in foreign people, letting them have the jobs and the houses that we have all been waiting for.

Sometimes I would walk down the streets in Alex and look at all the shops owned by Pakistanis and Nigerians. I would see those Mozambicans running hair salons. And I just knew, they're taking the money they make and sending it back home, while meanwhile there are South Africans all around them who are starving, who can't find a single job that will take them. It's a burden for us. It's not an easy thing. It's just not.

Still, my heart breaks sometimes for these people, the ones who just want a better life. There was a Mozambican man who used to sit on a corner not far from here, selling sweets and cigarettes. Every Sunday my mother and my granddaughter would walk past him on their way to church, and my granddaughter would say, 'Please *magogo*, can I buy some sweets?' And she would give her a rand or something for a Chappie.

But then in 2015, in April, I turned on the news one day and I was shocked. There were photos of this same man being stabbed by a group of *tsotsis*, right in the middle of the day, while people were watching. Right away, my granddaughter and my mother knew who it was. 'That's Sithole,' my granddaughter said. Emmanuel Sithole [also known as Emmanuel Josias]. A man who had been staying here for so many years. A quiet man. He just sat quietly. He didn't bother anyone. It made me so cold to think of this man dying in the street. So that was a criminal act. You can't call it xenophobia if people kill a man like that. It's just crime. They're just hooligans taking advantage of the chaos.

Since then, I've been thinking a lot to myself. What can we do now? This problem has gotten so bad. People are killing their black brothers and sisters – Africans like us. But at the same time, there is a real burden for us, the ones who grew up struggling, the ones who are watching those people all around us still struggling. There are people living in Alex who have a historical background here, who want to live and die here because that's what their families have always done. We cannot deny them this feeling, this wanting to belong in a place that is theirs.

It's not easy to be a leader now, at a moment like this. In actual fact, it's hard, really hard. It's so complicated.

4

JOHANNESBURG HUSTLE

Lucas Machel

AGE WHEN INTERVIEWED: **28**
BORN: Xai-Xai, Mozambique
INTERVIEWED IN: Tshepisong, Krugersdorp, South Africa
INTERVIEWED BY: Oupa Nkosi
PHOTOGRAPHED BY: Oupa Nkosi

Lucas Machel grew up in Mozambique, the son of a gold miner who worked in South Africa much of his life. Like many migrant workers, his father visited the family – his wife and four children – only during holidays. Machel, in his final year of school, got his girlfriend pregnant. In order to support his new family, he decided to quit school and follow his father to Johannesburg to make his way.

At home we were not poor and also not rich. Life was good. When I was still in primary school I would get everything because I was the first-born, so growing up I was very spoilt because I was the only child for a while. I remember when it was Teacher's Day, I was the most envied kid when it came to giving gifts to our teachers. Because my father worked in Johannesburg, I would always bring my teachers expensive gifts. I would bring them Colgate soaps and a hundred meticais. Back then it was big money.

Our school was not under government, it was privately managed, and the teacher was paid from our school fees. The school was made out of cane, with no proper classrooms, and every month people would come and fix it. We learnt under the trees. All the subjects were taught in Portuguese.

When I would come back from school my mother would be at work at the electoral commission. A helper was always there to assist me to bath, eat and do homework. Even though my mother only obtained a grade four certificate, every day when she arrived home she would first ask me: 'What did you do at school?' and after that, she would look at my homework. Then she would ask, 'What did your teacher talk about today?'

My mother was very strict and would discipline you if you were out of order. My father could not beat a child; he was the kind of father that will tell you straight that you don't beat a child. He preferred to sit you down and guard you.

RUNNING AWAY

When I got to grade eight, I had to move to Chibuto because there were no high schools in my village. I moved into my uncle's place and stayed with my aunt and grandmother. There, things became different. My aunt did not have kids of her own and she didn't treat me well. Let's say you were doing something, maybe in the kitchen, immediately when you leave, she will sweep the floor in order to prevent you from coming back. She would also accuse me of stealing and other sorts of things.

I felt okay at school but when it was time to go home, I felt bad. I eventually became demotivated at school and started to be naughty. One day I ended up slapping my aunt because she was rude to me. On that Friday, I did not go to school. I caught a taxi and went home to tell my mother what happened. My mother took me back to my aunt and talked to her about the issue. It was resolved and she realised that my aunt was wrong.

When I was in grade nine, I started flirting with this girl next door. When I was in grade ten, she fell pregnant. I accepted that I was the father of the child when her family brought her home. But I felt that

I was a burden to my parents then. They were now supporting the three of us: my child, my girlfriend and me.

In 2011, I decided I should go to Johannesburg to hustle and see what I can come up with. My mother did not agree with my decision; she was willing to support me until I finished school.

But I said, 'Mom, I'm staying with you here full-time and I can see that you are working but the money that you are making has become less and less. I don't know if Dad will allow me to go back to school.' So, I decided to run away to Johannesburg with money that I stole from my mother's purse.

After I crossed the border, I got in a taxi to Johannesburg and paid the taxi driver R270 without knowing for sure where I was heading. I did not have a cellphone, I only had a paper with the cellphone number of my cousin written on it. I called him when I arrived, but I had to lie to him by telling him that I was on holiday in order for him to receive me. He eventually agreed and gave me directions to his place in Orange Farm. I arrived late and spent the night, and the next day I confessed and told him I was a father and I wanted work to support my family. He asked about what my parents said about me coming to Johannesburg and I said to him straight that I stole my mother's money because she did not want me to come here, that she wanted me to go to school.

WORKING FOR THE WHITE MAN

Life on the farm was tough. My cousin was cutting grass for thatch roofing. He took me along, but the work was hard for me to do. Later, I asked him if he could talk to his boss to give me different work. The next day, we woke up early to get to the white man.

My cousin asked him if he could find me a job to do. The white man called me *manyambane* and asked if I could speak English. I told him that I'm not good, but I can try. He said to me, 'Then we will speak Fanagalo.'

I worked as a garden boy. The white man, Martin, also had cattle and I ended up taking care of them, too. Martin would buy me 12.5 kilogrammes of maize meal and every day would give me two litres of milk on top of my salary; I was first paid R2 200 and then R2 500 the next month.

His wife was kind to me and would give me extra money. She spoke in Afrikaans and it was my first time hearing such a language. She didn't like to speak English. Whenever she was giving me money, she would tell me not to tell the boss.

Martin did not treat me right but he never harassed me. I would tell him sometimes that I wanted to leave. I worked the whole day, and he did not want me to have a break. He wanted me to work non-stop. I would tell him, 'Come month-end, you would not see me.' He begged me not to leave.

I started work at 4 am finished at 6 pm. It was so cold in the morning – it was winter then – and his farm was very far from where we stayed. Sometimes on our way to work we would find dead bodies. It was very scary walking in the veld to get to his place.

I would milk the cattle, do the garden and later count the cattle and lock up and take the keys to him. I was hustling. When I was milking the cattle, I would have extra bottles that I would fill. A bottle of milk was R10. Sometimes I would sell ten bottles and I would tell him that I sold five. He did not notice because he was not even interested in this business. For him it was just extra cash. He also had chickens. I would also steal them.

Because it was my last month working with him, I was just messing things up. Month-end came, and I got paid. I always had to sign. '*Manyambane signa lapha. Manyambane* sign here.' I would sign and get my money. He would say, '*Ayi wena baleka. Mina cela wena buya kusasa.* Are you going to leave? Please come back tomorrow.' I told him, '*Mina bass ngizobuya.* I'm coming back, boss.'

But after two months I ran away.

I went to my father in Rustenburg and told him that I quit work. I gave him the money: R2 300. The next day, he took me to go buy clothes at the Jet store. After that he said to me, 'Because you failed to work, I'm going to give you money to go back home and go back to school.' I was fine with the idea. I was homesick. The next morning, I was in a taxi heading back home.

When I arrived at home, my mother was glad to see me. She said, 'I told you not to leave school. So, it is now up to you whether you still want to attend school or go back to Johannesburg.' I said, 'No Mama, I can no longer go back to school. I'm now old. Anyway, now that there is money available, please would you give me R500 to go back to Johannesburg? I will see and if things don't work out then I will go back to school.' She let me go.

WE ARE ALL AFRICANS

I went back to another uncle in Johannesburg, who had a hair salon. I started working with him, cutting hair and doing relaxing. At first I did not know how, but he taught me. I ended up being perfect at it.

I asked him, 'Uncle how much am I getting paid in a week?' He said, 'I pay you R200.' Every day he would only pay me R20 to buy bread. I lived with him for a while but then he hired a shack in someone's backyard and brought me everything I needed. He gave me a bed, pots, blankets, everything. I started to live on my own.

The owner of the house liked me. He thought I had the brain to think for myself, and also, because I was not naughty. He left me to look after his house when he went to live in a village in Nelspruit.

When I first moved in, I was paying R100 but when he left for Nelspruit he said I should only buy electricity. So I stopped paying rent at my leaking shack. The house was big and had three rooms. The problem was with some of my neighbours, the other Pedi tenants.

They saw my life was better than theirs so they had a problem with that. They did not even want to see me. They were saying, why is that I come from another country and I live a better life than them and that this country belongs to them. So sometimes I would tell the husband, 'We are all Africans. It does not matter whether I come from Maputo. The most important thing is that we respect each other as people.'

Their room had the main electrical switch in it so when the electricity was down the wife would not respond to my knocks and would only switch on my plug when she felt like it. Sometimes she would lock the outside toilet room. What made us fight a lot is when she demanded that I clean the outside toilet room more times than everyone else. Let's say, I would clean it this week and next week they would not. And I ended up cleaning the toilet again. So, they treated me in funny ways.

One day, the burglar bars in the yard which were about to be installed went missing. I was accused of stealing. It was hurtful to me because I don't take anyone's things without permission. If I want something, I ask for it or else I try to budget to be able to buy it. If I see that I cannot afford to have it, I just forget about it.

BECOMING A BRICKLAYER

After some time of living by myself, I fought with my uncle because of money. When I asked him about it, he would tell me that he was saving it for me. But I told him: 'Uncle, you know that I have a child back home. I need money to buy things.' Then he will promise me that he will give the money the next week, then next week and next week. I decided to leave him.

That was when I met Petros in Tshepisong. I approached him one Sunday morning and asked if I can work with him, even though I did not have enough skills. He agreed. The following morning I started work.

I was paid R90 a day for mixing cement. I did that for three days. Then one day – I remember we were in Meadowlands in Zone 8 – and I asked Lucky, the guy I used to mix cement for, if he could lend

me his trowel. I'd been observing all along how he was laying the bricks. Petros was present and he saw how good I laid the bricks. Then Lucky ended up mixing cement for me. From there, I started working as a bricklayer.

To me bricklaying is about love. I like it because there is a knock-off time and you don't get so dirty. You wait for the assistants to mix cement and pack bricks for you before you start working. You can arrive at the site at six in the morning you maybe start working around eight, but the assistants start to work immediately when they get to the site. That's how I fell in love with bricklaying.

THEY THINK I WON'T BE ABLE TO AFFORD SUCH THINGS

My life has changed since then. Back then when I used to mix cement, I lived in a shack. When it rained my shack will be filled with water. The only place where the water could not enter was where my bed was. I used to wear safety boots every time it rained. Now I can afford to live in a proper place. If I want to buy something that costs

R1 000, I can pay cash to buy it. If I want to buy something for R3 000, I lay-by it until I get it.

Like this fridge here, it's now three days old. I bought it brand new. I just bought it. When other people see me buying such things, they become jealous. I don't know what they think. Maybe they think that because I'm a Shangaan from Maputo, I won't be able to afford such things.

The other day I bought a big 15-inch plasma TV. I bought it cash from the old man in Kagiso, for R4 000.

In the yard, if you open the door, everyone wants to see what's inside. So, one day when I came back from work, I heard that the police had been there to investigate how I manage to own such a TV. At around two in the morning, I heard a knock on my door. It was the police, so I opened the door to let them in. My neighbours were also there and some of them were telling the police that they should take the TV.

The police searched the place and eventually asked where I got the TV. I produced the receipt and they said it was a false receipt. I had the old man's number. They demanded to take the TV but I refused. I told them that if this TV is stolen, they should take the serial numbers and call it in and if they find it stolen then they can take it. They tried several times phoning the old man but he never answered because it was still very early in the morning.

The neighbours wanted to see what was going to happen but they were disappointed. The police eventually left but promised to come back. They never did.

OPERATION FIELA

Following a spate of xenophobic attacks in April 2015, the government launched Operation Fiela – fiela translates as 'sweep clean' in Sesotho – which was ostensibly aimed at eliminating criminality and 'general lawlessness' but heavily targeted foreign residents in poor areas. At the time, Machel was working as a builder at a house in Soweto. An unmarked car filled with policemen stopped at the house and the police started chasing the workers. They all ran, jumping walls into neighbours' yards and hiding in outside rooms. Machel managed to flee, but many others were arrested and deported to their respective countries.

During Operation Fiela the police harassed us. But it was not only the police, even the community members at large were harassing us. They would swear at you or say nasty things like, 'Get out of here you Shangaan,' or even kick you. Police would demand passports and if found without one, *eish*! They would take you inside the police van like you are a piece of shit.

My colleagues would normally run away anytime they saw police, but I never did because at that time I had a valid passport and a permit. So, when people spoke ill about us, I would just look at them and do my own work without paying much attention.

But during that time, there were some police who followed a certain routine near our workplace. They usually came immediately after six in the morning, just after we arrived. Sometimes the owner of the house would hide us. Sometimes she would go talk to them and we would overhear her telling the police they should not come here to trouble us, that we are here to work and we never bothered anyone. She would tell them they could not come back to her yard without asking permission. But we were still terrified that they would come back and arrest us.

One time, my three friends from work caught a taxi and they were stopped by police. They were immediately spotted, out of many passengers. The police demanded to see their passports. They didn't have any, so they were taken out of the taxi and thrown at the back of the police van.

I guess they were easily spotted because Shangaan people dress in a particular way. They are easily identified. They dress poorly, as if they got the clothes from the dump. Most South Africans, even if they don't have money, they have a dress sense. Also foreign nationals, when they see the police, they become scared. They start to tremble. Most of the time it's like that.

At the end, the community started to also be xenophobic because one Somalian killed a child in Snake Park. If somebody steals from you, you don't solve that by killing him. They caused this mess. Anyway, things happen. We cannot decide for other people in their country what they should do.

IN SOUTH AFRICA, YOU CAN DIE ANYTIME

When I look at South African people, I no longer trust them. They are hot-headed. No matter how you can help or live in good standing with them, they end up stabbing you in the back. I no longer have faith in them. It's better that I live alone or with my own people. I tried to be nice to people that I live with or work with or meet on the streets, but the friendship does not end well.

Other foreigners from Nigeria, Malawi and Zimbabwe are fine – we are friendly to each other. I tried to live with the locals but they don't seem to be willing to live with us. There are some South Africans that are good people and I've tried asking them why others are behaving like this, and they tell me that it's how they were brought up and that's what's in their heart.

The thing that scares me is that some at first pretend to be fine and welcoming but later on they start showing their horrible, darker side. So, such things will make me kill someone or end up being killed. I no longer feel safe in South Africa because you can die anytime.

I WILL RETIRE AND GO HOME

Sometimes I evaluate my life and think about why I came to Johannesburg and what would life be like if I stayed back home. My parents never thought I would live here. They both hoped that I would finish school and teach or become an electrician. I also wished to be an electrician. When I see friends I went to school with, they end up buying me things. If I completed my studies back home, I would be living comfortably now. I would be not paying rent; I would live with my family and share everything. But I also don't regret because I'm grateful for what I'm doing and the money that I'm earning because I can do anything I want.

By now I have three kids, but I am expecting another child with my new girlfriend. I have two kids in Maputo, one in Springs and another one coming. My old girlfriend, who I have two kids with, used to stress me when it comes to money issues. She's from a rich family and used to demand a lot. I could not afford a lot of things and maybe she felt that I did not love her much. She said my money was going elsewhere and she eventually left.

So now I pay rent and buy food for myself but I share and I budget and send some money home. Washing soap, oil, green pepper, onion, meat, bathing soap – that's all very expensive back at home so I buy that and send it home. Meat here is cheap and I buy it and store it in a fridge so it's dry and send it back home in a cooler box.

Since I've started praying, things are better. Whatever I earn, I donate some to the church and in return God multiplies what I get. Petros now pays me more money. That's why I now devote my life to God. He only needs your heart, nothing else.

I pray to God to make me a business owner. I know lot of things in construction. I know how to build, plaster, mix cement and do roofing. But being an owner, you wake up whenever you wish and you make a lot of money. You charge clients and pay your workers a fee that you agreed upon and what's left, it's your profit.

Last year December I bought a stand back home for forty-five thousand meticais. Even when I'm old or dead, my kids will say that they are at their father's home. My plan is to build a three-roomed house that has a wall all around and open a tuckshop, so the mother of my kids can run it. I will continue to work and hopefully I can buy myself a van and a taxi for business. Then I will retire from Johannesburg and go back home.

5

DON'T. EXPOSE. YOURSELF

Papi Thetele

AGE WHEN INTERVIEWED: **48**
BORN: Carletonville, South Africa
INTERVIEWED IN: Katlehong, South Africa
INTERVIEWED BY: Caroline Wanjiku Kihato
PHOTOGRAPHED BY: Oupa Nkosi

Papi Thetele runs the Katlehong AIDS Council, a community-based organisation that provides support to women and children affected by HIV/AIDS. After the xenophobic attacks in 2008, Thetele introduced dialogues around the topic into his winter school programme. His story was recorded in a dilapidated township school, on Johannesburg's city streets in between meetings with potential funders and outside his two-and-a-half-roomed Reconstruction and Development Programme (RDP) house in Katlehong township, south of Johannesburg.

Why I do community work? I do not know. It is something in me, I don't think I can explain it. I have tried to explain it to myself but I have no answer. I was born a leader, inspired by people like Nelson Mandela, Archbishop Desmond Tutu, Steven Biko and Robert Sobukwe. I wanted to be like them. Maybe that explains why I am protective of everyone in the community. Community work chose me, I did not choose community work. As my mother would tell you, I was supposed to be a teacher!

LESSON 1: EVERYBODY SMELLS IN THE TOWNSHIP

In Thetele's class on a winter day in July.

'Now guys, today we are going back to basics. Remember PKK! *Phakamisa; Khomba; Khuluma!* Raise your hand; Let me point to you; Speak!'

PKK!

'Today we are speaking about other people in the townships. We live with Somalians, Ethiopians, Ghanaians and Cameroonians in the township, yes?'

'Yes!'

'Is there anything different about these people?'

'They take the body parts of young people and cut them up!'

'Oh wow! Have you actually seen this?'

'No, I heard about it.'

'Do you know if it is a South African or a foreigner doing that?'

'No!'

'Is it true?'

'Yes! Noooo! Yes? Nooooooo!!'

'We need to investigate the facts before we say that is true. Okay, what else?'

'They bring diseases like Ebola!'

'Do you know anybody who has Ebola in the township?'

'No!'

'Then that's a myth.'

'Foreigners are smelly!'

'Point me to somebody who stays in the township who is not smelly! We've got people who are smoking *nyaope* in the township. They are more smelly than the Ghanaian people! Even the Shangaans of this world, you get into a taxi with them and you cannot tell them "Your armpit is too smelly." So you cannot single the foreigners out. These are misconceptions and myths!'

Thetele's organisation started running its winter school in 2006. It now serves 120 schoolchildren in the Katlehong area.

I started the winter school because I noticed that so many babies were born from teenage mums around March and April in the township. When I did the calculation, I realised that most teenage pregnancies in the township happen in winter time, when schoolkids are on holiday and have nothing to do. Many of them are HIV/AIDS orphans and run child-headed households.

In the winter school, we take collective responsibility for kids who have to take medicines. We talk about the stigma of HIV/AIDS and how we can support each other. We teach life skills and civic education programmes and keep kids out of trouble.

Since the 2008 xenophobic attacks in Katlehong and other areas, I couldn't stand aside and see other people suffering. It was part of my upbringing to help people who had less than us. My mother and grandmother were very religious and they forced us to go to church. I remember in Sunday school they would teach us to say something if we see something wrong, to share what little bit we had with others who did not have. I left church after my mother passed on, but I have never forgotten the lessons I learnt.

So when the xenophobic attacks happened, I started focus group discussions and community dialogues to begin to say, is it okay for us as blacks to keep each other poor because some come from Malawi or Zambia or other countries?

As part of the winter school programme we talk about xenophobia and how it impacts our community. In our classes, the kids come up with all sorts of myths about foreigners. Some very extreme. But everybody in the township thinks about foreigners in these extreme ways. There are a lot of misconceptions and myths. So, in the winter school, we look closely at the issue and we dismantle the myths.

LESSON 2: HOW TO SURVIVE IN THE TOWNSHIP

In April 2016, foreign-owned shops were attacked and looted in Katlehong, in a neighbourhood close to Thetele's home. Many sought refuge at a nearby police station and waited until the violence had died down. Some foreigners fled the township completely in fear of their lives.

I normally say, once we can change the mentality of the Somalians and the Ethiopians, especially the people owning businesses in the township, there is a possibility of lasting peace. The last time we spoke to foreign nationals we said to them: Don't. Expose. Yourself!

We want to develop a concept document with the do's and the don'ts of the township.

One. You can't speak the language so the only way to get girls is through money. You splash out money like hell in taverns and the township boys are saying 'Oh, he's got money? How do I get that money?' Don't. Expose. Yourself.

Two. You go to a tavern – don't carry a laptop with you! You arrive in a tavern and you take your laptop out? Township life is not like that. You. Expose. Yourself.

Three. You've got an expensive phone? Put it on silent, put it in your pocket and you make sure that while you are with people, you don't answer your phone.

Four. You drive a nice car? Make sure that your windows are half closed. Don't open your window and start taking your elbow outside and asking for directions.

Five. If you are lost, use the GPS. If not, use the local police station. If not, use the garage. Why do you pass a church and ask the boys in the corner for directions? Why do you ignore the police station and go straight to those boys? Why? Take precautions! Make sure that you Don't. Expose. Yourself.

Six. If you move to the township, start engaging with the young people. Instead of going to taverns and splashing money why don't you join a soccer team? That is a safe space that you can create!

Thetele was born in 1968 at the height of apartheid repression in Carletonville, then a wealthy mining town west of Johannesburg. That same year, students at the University of Cape Town led a sit-in to protest against the apartheid government's interference in the hiring of the first black lecturer, Archie Mafeje. After nine days of student protest across the country, the students ended their sit-in. The university did not make a black appointment until 1980.

My uncle, my mum's brother, was one of the people that pushed me to study. He was tall and dark in complexion. He wore reading glasses and always carried *The Star* newspaper under his right arm. In those good olden days, we believed people wearing reading glasses were very educated. And he was, because he got a distinction in standard ten and went to university in the North West province. He was progressive, politically. He was a member of the South African National Civic Organisation that fought against apartheid and was also part of the Student Representative Council in school, which was the political student wing of the African National Congress.

My uncle had a stack of books in his room. He had many books; the most memorable for me was *I Write What I Like* by Steve Biko.

Every time I came back from school I would take one book and try to read it. Mostly I could not understand his English or Afrikaans books, but I read them anyway. He would encourage us to read anything that had to do with politics, so I was one of the active people in the household, reading. I remember waiting for my uncle to finish reading the newspaper. Immediately when he put it down, I would take it and read.

When I started working he came to stay with me. While I was growing up, my uncle was the breadwinner, he paid my school fees and school trips. He would give me the shoes and trousers that he used to wear, so that when I went to school I did not feel that I lacked anything.

So when he came to live with me a few years ago, I bought him a newspaper each day to repay him for all he had done for me. Shortly after coming to live with me, he was diagnosed as HIV-positive. I was an AIDS activist so I took him to my basic-introduction-to-HIV classes and I took him to my basic counselling classes; I had to teach him how to live a healthy lifestyle and how to adhere to treatment.

Unfortunately, it was during those times of AIDS denial in South Africa so we didn't get medicines from the government. We depended on hygiene, eating healthy meals and those kinds of things.

Seeing my uncle sick and losing weight was something hard to understand. It was very, very painful. We grew up knowing that parents took care of us young ones. To see someone who was powerful become so powerless and dependent was not easy for me. Now the roles were reversed and I, being the only AIDS activist in my home, became his guardian, taking care of him … it was difficult emotionally.

He passed on when he was staying with me here. I am not quite sure how old he was because you do not discuss age with an elder, you know. That was a taboo. But I think he was around 50. Very young when he passed on, but he had already achieved most of the things he wanted to when he was alive. He has six kids in Carletonville.

LESSON 3: LOCAL JUSTICE

In March 2016, violence broke out in Mandela Squatter Camp in Katlehong, not far from where Thetele lives. The shooting and injuring of three people by a Somali shopkeeper sparked the incident. In protest against the shooting, residents in the area looted 50 Somali shops. The Somali shopkeeper was charged with three counts of attempted murder and the possession of an unlicensed firearm.

I got a call. There was a shooting incident in Nkhapo section, in the Mandela Squatter Camp, and the residents were burning Somali shops in the area.

When I got there, I could see there were thugs involved in this incident, and not the community as a whole. Somebody within the township had sold a gun to a Somalian because the Somalian was being robbed on a daily basis. Three days later, the seller told his friends about the gun so that they could steal it from the Somalian and sell it to somebody else. When they went for the gun, the Somalian took it out and shot and injured two people.

In my understanding the mistake was, one: the person who sold the gun. He was the very same person who leaked the information to his friends and they were coming to rob them so that they could make more money from the gun. Two: the Somalian who admitted guilt and paid a bail amount of R3 000.

Why do I say this? I don't think Somalians will come all the way from Somalia carrying a gun. So why did they pay the admission of guilt? That was the mistake because the shooting incident was not the Somalian's fault, they were just defending themselves. Before the admission of guilt, we could have held deliberations as a community and we could have understood exactly where the cause of the problem was. We would have called the gun-seller to say, 'Can you see what you have done?' and dealt with it.

Now as a community we could not deal with this matter because the Somalian had already admitted guilt. And when they do that, the community says, 'You see, we told you that these guys were guilty, and we don't want them anymore in the township!' If we think that the matter is sorted out now because of the guilty plea, it is not. It will not stop the violence.

Thetele was raised by his grandmother in Carletonville. His mother, a domestic worker, had a job working in Germiston, almost a hundred kilometres away.

My mother was short, and outgoing. She would do anything to make sure her kids were protected. My grandmother was, however, a very strict person. So sometimes I would do a mistake and my grandmother would promise to punish me. The only safe haven I had was my mum. I would travel alone at the age of nine from Carletonville to Germiston on the train, just to see my mum. I would arrive at my mum past eleven in the evening and she would shout at me, but secretly I knew she was happy to see me. I would spend the night and the following day she would give somebody money and say, 'Take him back.'

I would get the punishment that I ran away from at my grandmother's the following day! But it was very touching because in my grandmother's house we were 15 grandchildren from different aunties and uncles. I normally tell my kids, 'You know when I was growing up the adults would dish out for the kids, and then they will dish out for the adults.' Also, we never knew meat when we were growing up. I only know meat now because I am staying alone.

I was very close to my mum. I am her last-born and the only person who would remember my mum's birthday. Every year, after she retired, come 20 August, I would celebrate her birthday with her, even if it was a small one.

My mum always wanted me to be a teacher, but when I chose community work, she still supported me. She supported me irrespective of what I did. She was one of the most motivating people in my life. I only got to start earning a salary five years before she retired. And until then, she took care of my kids and made sure that we had everything in the house. She kept the fire burning until she passed on four years ago.

LESSON 4: ON SOFT TARGETS

I think that violence is the historical culture of people in South Africa. If you look from the 1976 Soweto uprising up to now, every time people are dissatisfied with something they look for a soft target. I still remember when I was at school, every time we had an apartheid protest and there was a boer on this side and a bakery on another side, we will go for the bakery rather than go for the police. It is our historical background, and township people still continue with it; they have not diverted.

Let's define a soft target. A soft target is somebody I can just hit and they cannot go to the police station. I know very well that if I do that to a local person who knows me, he can go to the police station. And the police can come after me. But then how can the Somalians find me? Even if he saw you, he doesn't know where you are coming from! He doesn't know where you are staying! But a local person can automatically identify you. Somebody might say 'I know that guy; I don't know his name, but I know his parents.' So you see, the Somalians are soft targets because they don't have that knowledge.

Violence against foreigners is not because people in the township hate foreigners. No. It is because during that particular time when they are angry, say because of poor service delivery, they think, what can I do to make an impact so the government can hear me?

Unfortunately, Somalians are the soft targets in the picture at the time and that is why people go for them.

But even though I believe that it is not hatred of Somalians because of who they are, I still think it is important to admit that violence against them is xenophobia. Then we can sit down and ask ourselves, how do we protect the foreign people that are within us? It's a question of saying as long as you are a soft target coming from somewhere and you cannot report your case anywhere, then you are a target. If we don't say that it is xenophobic attacks, we will say 'these are individuals being targeted'. But then how do we then begin to protect individuals?

This thing, it does not happen to individuals! It happens to a particular group of people. And the minute it happens it is massive, it spreads! So, once we call it xenophobia we can address it.

Thetele has six children who live with their mother in Katlehong in a section on the opposite side from where he lives. He doesn't speak much about his relationship with his children.

I am not a hands-on father. My wife takes care of my kids. Much as I don't have much and my community work-life sometimes means I ignore my children, my love for them is unconditional. But I have got so many children to take care of at the camp and in the community. I believe that by helping others, my own children also benefit.

LESSON 5: LET US INTEGRATE

The last time we had a social cohesion event with the African Diaspora Forum in the township, they only told us that we should organise this event during the week because over the weekend, their members are busy because they are business owners.

We said to them, as much as you are business owners you are also part of the community. Very soon we will start seeing young girls chasing after the Somalians in the township, then we will start seeing Somalian children born by local girls. If you are not going to integrate, people will start making sure that when they attack you they will attack your kid as well. So, create a safe space. Integrate. Come to the meeting, soccer matches, leave your own football team, join these congregations in the township.

Integration should not be a one-sided thing where they come in when there is a funeral and just donate food and they go away. For me integration should be a day-to-day life kind of thing.

Somalians don't drink too much; they don't smoke too much; let them make sure from time to time they integrate and mix with the people. I can tell you, if that is a possibility, there is a possibility of lasting peace.

6

THE BIG MAN OF HOSAENA

Estifanos Worku Abeto

AGE WHEN INTERVIEWED: 72
BORN: Hosaena, Ethiopia
INTERVIEWED IN: Yeoville, Johannesburg, South Africa
INTERVIEWED BY: Tanya Pampalone
PHOTOGRAPHED BY: Madelene Cronje

Estifanos Worku Abeto grew up in the town of Hosaena, in the southern region of Ethiopia. The son of a farmer and his second wife, he got a job out of high school working for the local government in agricultural research. Later he studied botany at Haramaya University, returning to the civil service where he would stay for the next 35 years. In 1992, Worku Abeto joined the Ethiopian People's Revolutionary Democratic Front (EPRDF), a rebel coalition that seized power after years of fighting the ruling Derg, a military dictatorship that had ruled the country since it deposed Emperor Haile Selassie in 1974. In 1995, after multi-party elections, the EPRDF took power. Since then, international organisations have consistently condemned the party for political and media repression and massive human rights violations, including rape, murder and genocide.

When I met my wife, she was a student and I was working in the Ministry of State Farm in Awasa. She was 25 and I was 40. I first saw her in church, and she was just so beautiful. I went to her and said, 'Can you marry me?' And she said, 'Let me think about it.' I told my friend that I wanted to marry this girl so he went to contact her mother and father. When we went to her home, we found the food-and-drinks ceremony ready for us, and we ate too much and celebrated together, and we signed the agreement. They said I must buy a dress for her, with nice gold earrings and a necklace and a ring, and for the father and mother I must also buy their clothes for the wedding and pay for the ceremony. So, we were married. I built our house with a dining room, three bedrooms and a bathroom. I was a chief then. It was a nice life, except for the politics.

AND THEN THEY DISAPPEARED

In 1992 I was living in Awasa and was a member of the EPRDF. It was a big town with a population of over 60 000 and divided into 14 zones. I was doing experimental work in plant research at the time and the people in the area knew me; they knew my character. They knew I was Christian, that I don't drink and that I am a very intelligent person. So when the elections came, the EPRDF elected me as chief in that zone.

But, after many years of working for the party, I started to hate it. Some of my friends were in the opposition parties, some in the Southern Ethiopia People's Democratic Coalition and others in the Coalition for Unity and Democracy (CUD). They were arrested, and then they would just disappear. We knew they were killed. We knew the party members were raping women, that there was too much corruption and people were being arrested without any investigation.

I finally became fed up. The Constitution was saying one thing, but they were doing another. I tried to advise others in the party, telling them their policies were no good, that the people were hungry. But no one could be against Prime Minister Meles Zenawi. The ruling party had become a dictatorship.

At the time, I had a friend, Abebe, who I had known for more than ten years. He was in the EPRDF, but he was like me. We talked about what was happening. We said, 'How can we serve this party? Why are they doing this?' Some people liked what they were doing but we saw people were dying without reason. Then they took Abebe. I heard this from his family. They told me, 'We don't know where he is.' They killed him. And the same problem was waiting for me. That's when I decided I must go.

ENEMY OF THE PARTY

By then I was secretary of the party in the Hadiya zone, working in the government offices in Hosaena as a manager in the Ministry of Tourism.

Before the elections, I joined the CUD. I knew a lot about it, and I knew it was a safe party. They had a policy to give land to the people and they didn't want to kill anyone. They came to me and they said I must join them. They said, 'We will win the elections.' If the CUD won, I would be in a big position there. And they did win. The CUD won all of Addis Ababa but the EPRDF brought tanks and military into the city. They were shooting people in the CUD and the other opposition parties. We were devastated. The EPRDF would not give up control.

To save myself, to protect myself, I left my home and my family in Hosaena. How could they come with me? I was in hiding, moving around the country, staying with different friends. If the EPRDF security saw me, they would just shoot me.

In June 2007, I was staying 20 kilometres away from Hosaena, in hiding with friends. But I thought, maybe it is safe now; let me go see my family. But the security was watching. While I was walking to my home, a member of the government security and two police officers came toward me.

They said, 'You are Estifanos. We heard you left us. We have your information.' I put my hands up but they pushed me. They put me in handcuffs and were hitting and kicking me, shouting: 'You are the enemy of the party, so now you'll see. We will kill you.'

They took me to the police station in Lemorada, registered my name and arranged my statement. The police were saying to each other, 'This person is dangerous. We have to investigate him and then we will take action.' To 'take action' is the secret word, the police word. It means they want to kill me, and when I heard them saying that I knew I had to go.

It was an old police station, just a small room with a small window and wooden walls, with a wooden fence around it, and there were more than 30 prisoners there. About half were political prisoners, many from the opposition parties. Others were criminals. It was a dirty place, with small ants and bed bugs in the blankets. You just slept on the floor, eating communally with the others whose families brought them food.

I was in the police station for three weeks, waiting for my chance. I was watching, learning how to escape. Finally, one night at midnight, when the other prisoners and the police watchman were sleeping, I escaped. I was with another guy – we were helping each other to get out – and slowly we went to the window and opened it and jumped out. We ran into the eucalyptus-tree forest not more than 250 metres away, and he went one way and I went the other way – toward the border.

GOD ORDERED THEM TO HELP ME

I couldn't see my family before I skipped; I just had to go. I had no money, no papers, only the clothes I was wearing. It took me three days to get to the Moyale border so I could go into Kenya. I walked during the night or begged for a ride in a lorry – during the day it was too dangerous to travel.

There was a small river at the border, and also a forest. I crossed through the forest to the Kenyan side where I stayed with some other Ethiopians. I slept in their home, and they gave me some money to help pay for food and transportation and gave me a change of clothes. Then I travelled to Nairobi, and there I found a church and the people there helped me with money for transportation and with food. But then I heard the Ethiopian security people were there in Nairobi. Other Ethiopians who had lived there for many years told me, 'Take care; there are security here. They are patrolling, supervising people.' They said it was better if I left.

After 18 days I went to the Ugandan border, with people helping me all along the way. I travelled to Kampala where I found an Apostolic church and I stayed there, and the people there contributed money for me. They were helping me, too. All along the way, people were helping me, this is how it is. God ordered them to. I stayed there in Kampala for 23 days. I wanted to stay longer, but there weren't any jobs.

So I went to Tanzania, travelling on lorries that were transporting products, and I finally made it to Dar es Salaam. They speak Swahili there. You know, they hate the British, so they don't like to speak English. When I was first there, I asked one old man, 'Please can you help me? I am Ethiopian. Do you know any Ethiopians here?' He said there was one Somali lady nearby, so I went to her house, and she spoke Amharic.

Amina said I could stay with her. She was good lady. Her husband was Tanzanian, and they had three children – two daughters and one boy. Her husband was a rich person and they had a big house. I told her, 'I have nothing; I am a refugee.' She said, 'No problem. You are welcome. You will get food.'

Amina gave me a shirt and trousers, but she also warned me to stay inside: 'It's a problem if you are a foreigner here. The police will arrest you.' I stayed with Amina for one month, but then she said I must go to the refugee camp in Lilongwe, Malawi, so I could get food there.

I knew what was waiting for me at home. In that situation, you can't go home. If I went to a refugee camp, I thought, maybe I could get resettlement from the United Nations. If I told them my story, I thought they would help me. I thought they would give me a job, that they would give me an ID. I thought everything would be okay.

MANY PEOPLE WERE TALKING ABOUT GOING TO SOUTH AFRICA

Located 25 kilometres north of Lilongwe, the Dzaleka Refugee Camp was opened by the United Nations High Commissioner for Refugees (UNHCR) in 1994, following the Rwandan genocide. Located along the migrant route to South Africa, it is estimated to host more than 25 000 people from the Democratic Republic of the Congo, Burundi, Rwanda, Somalia, Ethiopia, Mozambique, Zambia and Zimbabwe.

When I went to the refugee camp, there were many, many people, thousands of people, from different countries. I was talking mainly to the Ethiopians; they were escaping from the same problems as me – the political problems. I hated it there. There was malaria, and the food was giving the people dysentery. I was thinking how I was living a good life before, not this life. When I had my government job, life was better. I kept asking myself, where should I go?

Many people were talking about going to South Africa. I knew the history there. People were saying, 'If it is possible, go to South Africa. It's democratic. It's safe. No problem.'

So I left Malawi and went through Mozambique to get to South Africa. I arrived at the border in November. There are brokers there, you know, the human traffickers. At the border in other countries in Africa, no problem, you just walk across. But Tanzania and South Africa are very strict. Here, you need help.

I met an Eritrean guy in the border town who knew the crossing. He charged US$200 to take me across with eight Somalis and four other Ethiopians. We crossed at night. It was dangerous: there were many snakes and hyenas there in the forest. But the broker was guiding us. And God helped me. The broker told us how to go under the wire fence, and we pulled it up and passed underneath. On the other side of the border was a small lorry with no windows, just a canvas on the back. The driver told us all to get inside, and he gave us a warning. He said, 'Don't talk.' So we kept quiet and slept until we came to Johannesburg.

EVERYTHING IS GOING TO BE OKAY

After we passed the border, my mind got a bit of rest. The driver dropped us in downtown Johannesburg, in Jeppestown, and told us where to find the other Ethiopians. Some of them knew me because I was in a big post in Hosaena, and they offered for me to sleep in their house that night. The next day, I found my friend Asafa's phone number, who I knew from Ethiopia. Asafa was nearby, in Yeoville, and he told me, 'Don't worry. You can live with me until you get on your feet.'

After one week in South Africa, I phoned a friend in Hosaena and asked if he could tell my wife that I was in South Africa and that I was safe. A month later, I called again and my wife was there at that house. She was crying and weeping. But after a while, she was happy and she shouted, 'You are not dead! I thought the government killed you!' They all celebrated – my wife and my three children – they were all jumping.

She told me that when I left police were going to our house, that they arrested her. She told them she wasn't in a political party. She said, 'If you want Estifanos go find him.' But they kept her for a week in the police station. She was arrested because of me! Her friend, who was in the party, told the police that my wife was not political. She said, 'Find her husband.' And finally they let her out.

In Yeoville, Asafa introduced me to some other Ethiopians, and that's where I met Temesgen and Yosef. They were selling comforters and blankets, and they had a business for a long time. They said I could work with them because I knew how to write.

In February, we all decided to open a shop in Tsakane. I was thinking everything was going to be okay. I thought, I'm going to open the shop and send money for my family.

A South African lady owned the main house, and our shop was just beside hers on the street. We had the shop in the front and the three of us slept in the back – you know, many foreigners are living like this. It's normal, the shop in the front and sleep in the back. There were many other foreign shop owners in the area – Ethiopians, Somalis and Pakistanis. They all had tuckshops or clothing shops; some were going house-to-house selling blankets or coats, all different things.

The South Africans were all buying things at our shop. Sometimes there were thieves that would come in and the landlady would tell us, 'This guy is a thief.' But we didn't have any problems with the South Africans. The neighbours respected the landlady, so they were not making any problems for us.

THESE PEOPLE ARE COMING TO KILL US

The attacks happened on 19 May 2008. The night before, the community people were warning us. They came to the shop and were dancing and singing, saying, 'You foreigners, you must go back to your country! What are you doing here? This is our money! This isn't your money!' They were terrorising us. 'You *kwerekwere*, we'll show you!'

We didn't sleep that night. Though we were very scared, we couldn't leave. We were thinking these people would come and kill us. But the South African lady came to reassure us. She said, 'Don't worry.'

The next day, very early in the morning, they came in groups, singing. They went to all of the foreigners in the area. The three of us were hiding inside the shop, and they came en masse and broke down the door. The police were there, too, and they tried to protect us but there were too many people and they couldn't stop them. The community people were warning the police. They were warning them, saying: 'Take care. This is South Africa. We are South Africans.'

The landlady was crying. 'I'm South African. What are you doing?' They screamed, 'Where are the foreigners?' They were grabbing us, beating us, kicking us. We acted like dead people. The lady screamed, 'Are you killing me? Are you killing them?'

Then they left, taking the blankets, the comforters, the bedsheets, the carpets. They even took our cooking oil. Then they went to the money. We had R80 000 cash. They took everything we had. Then they broke the owner's house.

After they left, the police took us to the police station in Tsakane and we opened a case and listed everything that was looted. They gave us a case number, registering everything we said but they told us they couldn't do anything. They said, 'This is the community. What shall we do?'

THE ENEMY

The police took us to go to the UNHCR camp, which was set up in Springs. There were more than 300 or 400 people staying there by then. We ended up staying there for five or six months, living in tents, and they gave us food, clothes and blankets. It was very comfortable. I thank South Africa for this.

In the camp, I helped to coordinate the people. The Ethiopians elected me and, with the guys from Malawi and the other Zimbabweans, we were arranging the queues and the donations that were coming in.

Many different politicians came to the camp. They said, 'Don't worry. Be patient.' The white politicians [from the opposition Democratic Alliance] said, 'Maybe you will go to another country.' The African National Congress (ANC) politicians were saying, 'You must integrate.' They told us those people who attacked us were in prison. But those people were not in prison; it was not true. They were saying that just to comfort us.

The people in the camps were refusing to integrate back into those communities. How could we integrate with the South Africans? We didn't have anything. Everything we had was stolen. We were afraid; we were saying, 'How can we leave here? They are the enemy. If they see us, they will kill us.'

But after the politicians came, the camp was closed and the few of us who were left were taken to another camp.

I remember very well one man, a Rwandan from the United Nations, who spoke French. He said he could help me because I was a gentleman. But he was only helping the Congolese. He was a corrupt person. He was taking money. But I had none. He said, 'Don't worry, I'll help you.' But he didn't help me. Only God helped me.

Worku Abeto stayed in the second camp for another four months until it, too, closed. Those remaining were moved to a hostel in Rosettenville, until sometime in 2009. When it was closed, Oxfam, which was supporting the hostel, handed out R3 000 for rent and food to assist the displaced to set up a new life. Worku Abeto headed back to Yeoville, where he still lives. Since the attacks, he has been actively involved with the diaspora community, including the African Diaspora Forum which was set up in 2008, following the attacks.

Worku Abeto often represents Ethiopians living in Johannesburg in matters with the government.

THEY DIDN'T NEED ANY FOREIGNERS IN SOWETO

There were xenophobic attacks in Soweto again in January 2015, and foreign shops were looted for one month. The Soweto community then said they didn't want any foreigners in Soweto. There was one lady, Mama Rosa, who wrote a report for the small business minister. I went to Pretoria to represent the Ethiopians, but there were also representatives from Somalia, Pakistan and Bangladesh.

We had a three-day meeting in the minister's office so we could hear the report and give our feedback. They had the report taped to the wall, and after two days, they asked us, 'What do you think about this? What are your ideas? What are your objections?'

I raised my hand – there were representatives from many offices, from Home Affairs, from Social Development, more than 20 staff and one white lady taking minutes – and I said: 'How can you take this rubbish? Let me tell you something. I'm older than all of you. Maybe you have more knowledge, but you do not have more experience than me. You South Africans were foreigners in many countries. Mandela was in Ethiopia. He was a foreigner. Mandela went to the Ethiopian government and they gave him military training.'

We were helping them. But South Africans don't know about this history. They didn't learn about African history in school, but they were listening eagerly to what I was saying. I told them, 'Please, how can you say you don't need foreigners? Foreigners are everywhere. This is a shame to say that no one can enter Soweto.'

In the end, the move to ban foreigners from operating shops in Soweto was dismissed.

A LIFE OF SLAVERY

You see, my people are business people. They are peaceful, and they like to work. In Ethiopia, it's more like the white system. This is how they do it: they build shops, make houses, eat simple bread, give credit to customers and collect money at end of the month. They earn nice money this way.

But they got their businesses here by many sacrifices. With the robbers and the thieves in South Africa, they face many challenges. Some die by knives and others by shootings. Many, many have been killed. The *tsotsis*, they shoot you and take your money. The South Africans see we have a car, and they see this *kwerekwere* and they just want to hijack us.

I know some Ethiopians who live here for 15 or 20 years and they don't like to employ South Africans because South Africans don't like to work. They get tired and they go home early. The Zimbabweans and the Malawians? They work very hard. But if you employ a South African lady she will only ask for money. She doesn't want to work. If a South African man is working in a shop for six months or one year, he will ask compensation to leave the shop. But the shop can't pay that money. Maybe in a generation they will change. You see, apartheid was very clever. It paid people money every week, but then they would finish their salary and just wait to get paid again. The South African people don't work for the long run. It's the apartheid system. They don't like their people to be strong workers, to live long lives. They just enjoy the moment and then finish their money. But this is a life of slavery.

I NEED RESETTLEMENT

After living in South Africa for nine years, the only documentation Worku Abeto has is an asylum-seeker permit. The six-month permit is meant to be a temporary document which, by South African law, should be resolved by either rejection or by granting refugee status, the gateway to permanent residency. However, as the United Nations noted in 2016, South Africa has the highest number of unsettled asylum-seeker claims in the world. Worku Abeto is a case in point: he has renewed his temporary document more than 12 times.

The problem in South Africa is the permit. If I am a permanent resident of South Africa, then I can go home to Ethiopia to visit. They won't be able to arrest me because then I would be a South African. But I don't even have a passport. I only have a temporary asylum permit, which is supposed to last for just six months. For nine years I have a six-month permit. For nine years!

What I need is resettlement. I would like to go to America or Canada. If I were American, I could go to Ethiopia. Then government cannot touch you. It's no problem, you can visit or you can call on your families to come to stay with you. How can I call for them to come here now? If I were a citizen of South Africa, I could call them. But I'm not. If I had had R5 000 or R6 000 or R10 000, then I could get the permit. But if you don't have cash, then no permit. Without money, you can't do anything. Some people get the two-year refugee permit but they pay someone for this – this is corruption, this is how it works. But when the person goes back for their renewal, their permit isn't in the system – their information has been deleted. The people working at Home Affairs, they take your money. But sometimes this corruption is okay. You pay and they put you in the system and it's not deleted. Sometimes, they can put together the legal and the illegal and you can have your permit. No problem.

They keep rejecting me. But they cannot reject my case! I was a member of the ruling party! What is waiting for me there at home? Why did they reject me? They don't recognise who is who. Their meaning is this: go back to your country.

I am booked for an appeal hearing soon. This is supposed to be the final decision to deport me back to my country. I didn't leave for nothing. I left for a problem. They have to understand this. I love my family, my wife. Why would I leave there if there were no problems? But these people are crazy. I told them everything. They interviewed me many times. If they try to deport me, I won't go. I will go into their prison. If I go to my country, I will die. If I go to prison here, I will be able to live another life.

THE WORST LIFE

Now I stay in a flat here in Yeoville. Pastor Desta, he is Ethiopian, and has two churches. He is giving me money to help with rent and so I stay with him in a small room with two other Ethiopian guys. I can't exist this way. How can I live like this? For how long?

At my age, I know many things. When I was in government work, I was a big boss. I had many privileges. Now it is the worst life. If I think of this, my tears will come.

For money, sometimes I represent people, as an interpreter or if they are fighting with the police or there is a xenophobic problem or if they are fighting each other. Every day there are disagreements between Ethiopians, between the people, and they call me for peace-building because I am an elder. This is my work.

At my age, I can't find another job. I ask people, 'Why don't you employ me?' My mind is okay. I can work if I get any job. The problem is who is going to give me a job? They say, 'You are old. We cannot employ you. We need a younger person.'

IT'S FOR NOTHING

Let me tell the truth. South Africa is like prison for me. Prison means you cannot meet family, friends. You cannot relax. I can do nothing now. I'm an educated person. You have to understand the problem. If you are not visiting your family, your friends, what is the use of living alone here? Life is with family. So I'm still here, for nine years. I'm alone. You can't forget your family. If you are not Christian, then you can have a girlfriend or a boyfriend. But I am Christian. I cannot do this.

I love my children. I love my wife. I love her. What should I do? How can I help her? How can she help me? It's so long since I have seen my children. When I came here they were very small – the youngest was seven when I left. But I have not talked to them for a long time. How can I? I have nothing to send them. I can do nothing. My daughter now is completing university in Hagere Mariam, studying management and economics, and the next son is getting a doctorate at Hawassa University. My youngest son is in the ninth grade.

My wife's family is supporting them. Her brother and sisters are educated; they are government workers. They know I am nothing here. They say, 'Why don't you come home?' But how can I, with the politics there? As soon as I go there, they will arrest me.

At the time I escaped, I wanted to protect myself. Now I have been protected from that regime. But it is for nothing. Even if you are dressed nice, it's for nothing.

7

DO WE OWE THEM JUST BECAUSE THEY HELPED US?

Kopano Lebelo

AGE WHEN INTERVIEWED: 55
BORN: Pretoria, South Africa
INTERVIEWED IN: Pretoria, South Africa
INTERVIEWED BY: Thandiwe Ntshinga
PHOTOGRAPHED BY: Madelene Cronje

Kopano Lebelo grew up during apartheid in a township near Pretoria where, when he was still a teenager, he was drafted by the African National Congress (ANC) to recruit others in the struggle. Through his work with the ANC, he lived, studied and worked in various countries on the continent and in Europe, later studying for his master's degree in the United States. Since 2001, Lebelo has lived in suburban Pretoria with his teenage daughter, and is largely disengaged from formal political activism.

I regard myself as one of the lucky ones, exposed to fighting for liberation at an early age. It took away my childhood and my youth, which I didn't enjoy much, but the ANC moulded me and made me what I am today. I go back to the township now and I look at the people I grew up with and not even one can identify me as somebody that they know. All they think is, please can you buy me booze or give me a few bucks? I see myself through them and think, well, this is me if I hadn't gone out of the country.

There were six of us in our family. I have three older sisters and two younger brothers. After my parents passed on when I was very young, my uncle's family came to stay with us, so there were about 11 kids in that house in total. It was only when I came back from exile that I found out that the couple who raised me as their child – the only parents I knew – were in fact my uncle and aunt.

Growing up, my friends only saw life as it goes day by day, so when I started school I didn't see why I had to go. Not that I had much of a choice. But, at the age of 11, I started to go to the Zwartkop golf course, following some of the older kids who would go and get pocket money there as caddies. My parents didn't approve but I went anyway.

Later, I ran away and joined my friends, staying for about five months under Zwartkop Bridge between the R101 and Hans Strydom Drive, right next to the golf course. There was one old man who was a caddie master who used to tell us that you will not learn how to speak Afrikaans and English if you stay at home. He said the best way to learn how to speak like the white people is to stay with them; work with them. As an 11-year-old I believed that, so I stayed. The older kids taught me how to survive.

But it was not safe there. If you had some money, somebody would fight you for it. So you must hide it or use it. I didn't drink but I smoked glue and marijuana. The group I was in with meant I had to quickly learn how to make a *zol*.

My parents didn't know where I was until they found me, months later. At that time, corporal punishment was the in-thing so I had my own corporal punishment at home as well as at school, for not going to school.

My parents tried, but I just did not listen. I don't know how many times I was caned. They would make sure I would get to school. They would drop me off and pick me up. But I had friends who didn't go to school, so during break I would go join them. I was just a naughty teenage boy. At the time, I did not see any use or need for education. I just thought: I can survive, I know how to survive, I know how to basically look after myself.

For a long time, I was the last one in the class, not passing well. But then I felt like I needed to surprise everyone so I joined a group that studied at night, thinking, let me just try, and I passed well. Then I started studying and being like other kids and was identified as somebody who had the guts to stand up for himself on the struggle. That was when I was recruited with five of my friends to join the ANC.

SAVED BY THE ANC

The ANC wanted us to form cells, so I had to get a group of ten people who I would teach about the Freedom Charter and ANC policies and then those ten people would also get trained, and they would recruit ten more people, and that was how the movement would spread. At that time the biggest thing going was the 8 January speeches of Oliver Tambo. The ANC recruiters would make them available on cassettes and I would distribute them and talk about what the ANC was broadly about and make them aware that there were many ways to fight in the struggle, including taking up arms.

I always gave reports to the ANC on everything I did. They used to send people to come and collect information or give me information. They even gave me funds to do most of these mobilisations, and I started learning more and more.

Some in the township would tell me they had been fighting for a long time but they were not seeing any progress. They wanted to get out of the country and train to take up arms and fight against the situation in South Africa. Those were the ones who wanted to leave, and I just handed them over to whoever was sent by the ANC, mostly uMkhonto we Sizwe (MK) cadres, and they took them out of the country. There's a lot of people who went through that channel.

I was taught the road to take people out, to show them how to be taken into frontline states, and then come back and live normally, as if nothing had happened. In exchange for that the ANC had education in mind for me. They changed me from a street kid into somebody who cares for education; they identified a tutor who would teach me every night.

THE GATES WERE CLOSING ON US

One time I had a comrade who was supposed to leave the country, but a day later he came back and said that it was unsafe for him to leave. First, he didn't tell his parents he was going and second, he wanted to complete his matric.

But by then he had already seen things that he was not supposed to see. Later I learnt that just before they arrived at the border he decided he wasn't going, that he was scared or something. The ANC threatened him, saying if he went back he would be, you know, targeted by the MK, that something bad would happen to him. His mandate was not to talk. I told him the same thing – they taught us how to scare them – that should he ever say anything to anybody, his life would be ending.

He went back to the police and reported that he was unsafe and he wanted to be protected. Without even knowing, he had already brought the police to me. The police started to send every Jack and Jill on the road to come to me and say, 'Listen, I heard so-and-so left, can I also leave?' Again, I don't decide; I report. I used to report that all the time, almost every week.

Then the ANC advised me that, no, it was now dangerous for me to stay. We were just told on one day that we had to leave – now. There were five of us. I told them, 'Listen guys, we are meeting at this place; we are leaving now. No excuse. If you stay, then you are on your own.'

You can't wait for anyone. I mean, the gates were closing on us. I had just a little schoolbag to take with me. That was in August 1979.

BANISHMENT

Lebelo crossed the border into Swaziland, where he stayed with a university lecturer, and then moved into ANC-owned flats in Manzini for one month of training on military intelligence strategy and the tactics of MK, the military wing of the ANC. From there, he was taken to a camp in Mozambique.

You stay in the camp, you don't go anywhere. You go anywhere – Mozambicans do not speak English – and they'll shoot you. Then we were given two options: go to Tanzania for school or Angola for military. I decided to go to school.

In Tanzania, I lived in Mazimbu village in Morogoro, which was the place for ANC exiles to live. The ANC, with the help of sponsors, built a school called Solomon Mahlangu Freedom College. But we could not go anywhere. We were controlled, first by the ANC authorities, then by the local Tanzanian militia. Only if you were sick could you be taken to a doctor outside. The only Tanzanians we saw were the people that would come and work, or people that would do our services for us, or villagers around the area. At no stage was there anybody moving away to the middle of nowhere.

The issue of saying we were looked after in those countries? It's neither here nor there. It's nowhere. Yes, the frontline states were attacked by the South African military. But they also had their own struggles against South Africa. For example, Mozambique had to be militarised because South Africa was supporting the rebel group, Renamo, against the elected government. In many of the countries in Africa we were staying in camps. In Tanzania, we were living all in camps. In Angola, all in camps. Nothing to do with freedom. We were just there to do our job and our job was to train to fight against the system of South Africa. Nothing else.

Today our African brothers want to claim that there was an unwritten agreement that after the struggle we had to pay back by accepting economic refugees. But all living South African freedom fighters returned home to build their country.

There are so many people that came back into the country as South Africans but they are not South African, and we allowed that. Those were exceptions, those were the people that we lived with and their lives were just like ours. Those I can talk about, but not economic refugees. We were never economic refugees. We were never there to make money. We were there for a purpose and once that purpose was done we came back.

In 1982, Lebelo received an academic scholarship to study electronic engineering in Bulgaria, where he earned his first master's degree. He stayed in the country for much of the next eight years – with a stint in Greece where he was undercover for the ANC as a student – working as a miner, a DJ and a break-dancer. In 1990, the ANC finally provided Lebelo with a ticket to come closer to home, to Zimbabwe.

The Zimbabwean government did not fully support the ANC. Their ideology supported the Pan Africanist Congress of Azania (PAC), who say they will fight for Africa to remain for Africans. When I got there, I was banished to the house of one comrade; that's why I say we were not treated well in these countries. I still have the document that says, 'This is where you are restricted to stay; you are not supposed to move anywhere, you are supposed to stay in this house under house arrest.'

LISTEN, I NEED HELP

When I came back to South Africa, I lived with my sister in the township. We were given an allowance of about R800 every month. This was our first time getting an allowance, other than the small stipend given while studying. I didn't even know how to use it. If I got it, I gave it to family. I didn't need anything. I was already used to living

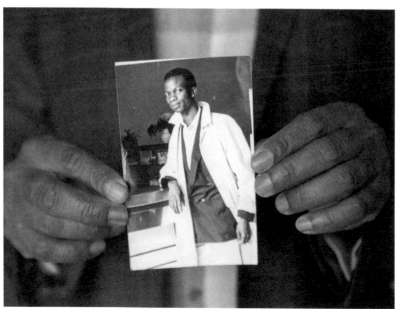

103

with what I have. Once in three months, six months, we would be given a new, second pair of trousers. It was not the priority, and when I was there [in exile] I did tailoring because we had to find skills to help each other, you know? When somebody found pants but they were too big somebody would tailor them. Some of them you would have to make yourself and sew from the beginning so I learnt to do that. Just like others would do carpentry, and others would do mechanics.

But with the family there were starting to be problems. My brother-in-law was saying I must join him to do garden work for his boss on the weekends. I have fought against the boers and now I must do garden work for them? But if I didn't work then he would take it personally.

I went to the ANC to ask for help. They said, 'Okay, we can pay for your corrugated irons and steels, then you can go build yourself a shack.' So I went to Orange Farm and built myself a shack there and stayed there for a few months.

In Christmas 1993 the ANC sent a message that said there were some white companies looking for engineers. They sent me to the German communications company Siemens, and they took me to the IEC – the electoral commission – where I was responsible for the telecommunication network for the 1994 election.

While I was still settling down at Siemens, the ANC said they wanted Armscor transformed so I must go and present myself at the arms company. The company gave me an offer. But I was undermined by those people. I was taken through interviews and they asked me how much I wanted, so I told them R100 000. I found out a few months later that that was way, way, way down. My senior manager felt bad for me and said that he had to make it double because he felt guilty.

Armscor sent Lebelo to the United States to study systems engineering at a naval postgraduate school. Since his return to South Africa in 2001, he has been working for the Department of Defence, where he is chief of procurement.

THOSE PEOPLE MUST GO TO REFUGEE CAMPS

Our neighbouring countries are taking advantage of the situation in South Africa. Their economies are struggling and they bring their unemployed or people who seek to survive to South Africa.

It's easy to go to South Africa illegally. In other countries you are asked to provide proof that you are able to maintain yourself over a period of time. They say in South Africa it takes R200 a day to survive and if you don't have that, then it's hard for you.

Zimbabwe just lets the people go. There's no control at the borders. They are allowed to leave and come here and transfer their problems to South Africa. And when they are here they take any job to survive – even if they are paid below minimum wage. That is what is killing the economy because economies are based on controls, and there are conditions of work that are determined. They can be paid nothing and work almost like slaves. It's not fair for them, and it's not right for the economy.

Why don't the Zimbabweans form a formal group which can go and address their issues in their country and see who will support them? South Africa can support them economically by saying okay fine, we will support those who are suffering, who don't have anything to eat, but those people must go to refugee camps. And they must be kept there and be looked after and counted so we know how many people are there and where they are from. They must be given their own IDs and records, which are not only available to us but also to the United Nations and their own countries. When all is right they must be able to go back home.

I feel for the situation that the other citizens find themselves in, but I blame their countries for not looking after their people.

Our economy has gone even worse than it was during the apartheid system. People in townships are destitute. There is no money. Hospitals are crowded because they cannot discriminate against other African refugees. So now you compare South Africans with people coming from other countries who must go and wait in a hospital for the whole day just to get attention? Our people will go but we won't wait the whole day. They are proud. They will fight and say, 'Why am I waiting the whole day?' But there is a long queue with people from outside and the hospitals are catering for anybody. Our medicine? The hospitals are running short of medication most of the time because they cater for anybody that comes into hospital.

You go to any country, whether it's in Europe, America or Asia; whether it's in Africa, there's no free-for-all. But we are catering for people that are not in our budget and it won't work. It will never work. In any country it will not work and it should not work here in South Africa.

We have meetings between all our government departments but when people try to talk about the issues, they are threatened with not being humanitarian enough, not being international enough, not being thankful for having been helped in the struggle.

Then you must pay Russia! Then you must pay China! You must pay Bulgaria! All those countries that we've been in. They are not demanding! Why are these countries in Africa demanding for hosting us? Then there are the people that never had anything to do with our struggle, those people from Pakistan, from Bangladesh.

There are other illegal immigrants coming from China, from Eastern Europe, and they are roaming freely here in the country. They are coming like refugees from everywhere. But the government is only worried about the blacks that are coming here – which they are not doing anything about.

I understand South Africans that take to the street because they feel that our government is not doing enough. It is totally not doing enough to address the issues that affect every one of us. The government is scared the United Nations will look at them in a bad way, but is the UN looking at America for what the Americans are saying about foreigners? Is the UN saying anything? No.

8

LOVE IN THE TIME OF XENOPHOBIA

Chichi Ngozi

AGE WHEN INTERVIEWED: 30
BORN: Owerri, Imo State, Nigeria
INTERVIEWED IN: Sunnyside, Pretoria, South Africa
INTERVIEWED BY: Ragi Bashonga
PHOTOGRAPHED BY: Madelene Cronje

Chichi Ngozi's childhood dream was to become a nun, a lifestyle choice her parents would never allow. Instead, she studied education in Owerri, in the heart of Igboland where she was raised. At the age of 24, a twist in an intimate relationship pushed her toward a new life in South Africa. She now lives in the suburb of Sunnyside in Pretoria with her husband and three-year-old daughter.

You know, here in South Africa, if you wear white clothes you can wear it from morning 'til night and even the following day, and if you decide not to wash it you won't wash it. But in Nigeria, you can't wear white because the dust is too much. The heat is too much. It's very, very hot. And we usually have electricity problems. You know, we say 'NEPA take light' – that's the power company – when our electricity goes off. You can bath in the morning and when you come back you have dust on your legs. You come home and you start washing, cleaning shoes. Here in South Africa you can go out in the morning and come back in the night and even if you don't feel like bathing, you will not bath because you will not be feeling the heat.

And the way they are dressing here is totally different from Nigeria. There, when you walk the streets wearing a miniskirt you feel embarrassed. They'll be shouting, 'Hey! Didn't your mother see you when you left the house? You want to show all the men that you are *ashawo*?' That is the word for a loose woman. You will feel so embarrassed!

Here you just mind your own business and you can wear anything you want. The most a boy can do is to whistle at you or hoot the horn in the car. But in Nigeria they can even be throwing water at you when you are walking. I'm telling you. There are so many things South Africa does better than Nigeria.

It's just that if you don't have money, *yoh*! You will die in South Africa! And you need to be very hard-working. If you are not hard-working you will end up in the street being a seller, selling your body up and down.

GROWING UP IN IGBOLAND

I grew up in Nigeria in Imo State in a very big city – the capital city, Owerri. When you have good money, you can go there to stay. It's where people come to spend, rest and eat some of their money. You can go out to eat, there are lots of pools, a lot of football – even a stadium where they do many sports.

There are a lot of Igbo people there in Imo State, like me, but there are different tribes of people as well – all Nigerian – and you will find up to 300 different languages spoken. I know a lot of people from other tribes: Yorubas, Hausa, Ganna and Ikota Epeni. I can also understand Yoruba because I spend a lot of time with Yoruba people.

I'm the fifth child of 11 children – two boys and nine girls. We're a Christian family. One father, one mother. No different parents. In our family we don't know anything about extended family – you know, like different mother, different father. There's nothing like that. My daddy was a medical doctor, but he's late now. My mother has a shop where she is selling provisions, food stocks, edible items, that sort of thing. She was doing that even before she gave birth to me. My mommy, she loves people. She is just the type that likes accommodating people, having a lot of people around.

When I was still a child, one of the things that I liked most was cultural dancing. In our place there was a time they would come for this traditional thing, they call it the Ozuru Imo festival, or Imo Day. Different tribes would come for their cultural dance and in our group I was one of the best dancers! My dream was to be a reverend sister, a nun, but my parents said they would never allow me to do that, even for one day. Education was the course the school gave me to read, even though really what I liked best was physical education and health. But I didn't really have any options, so I studied at the Alvan Ikowu College of Education, but when I finished it was not that easy to get a job. Finally, I just got work as a waitress in Owerri – a nice job but it wasn't in my profession.

IN LOVE WE ARE NOT PERFECT

I was at university and I was thinking the person I'm into is the person I'm going to spend the rest of my life with. It was…I won't say it's a rape. I won't say that. Why did he do it? It was a friend who misled him. I was still a virgin when I was with him. I gave him my pride, my honour. When someone takes your pride, you have nothing. I felt like the world had ended. I felt like cutting myself.

What happened was, his friend was saying, 'Maybe this girl is just pretending to be in love with you but is going out with other men.' That is why he did it, just to find out that I really know nothing about men. By then he was very sorry. He was always calling me, begging me, but I didn't even listen. Then I went back home, but I didn't even tell my parents what was going on.

So, what will I say my problem is? Why didn't I tell my mother? She tried a lot, she used to sell at the market, she used to do everything to make sure she takes care of us; you can see the way your mommy will be hustling for you. But as the grown girl you are, you associate in a relationship that you know can bear good fruit tomorrow. But in love we are not perfect. No one is perfect on this earth.

But it was very, very painful, sweetheart, the reason I left my home to come here.

I found out from a friend that this man, he impregnated another girl. You know it's better when someone tells you something like that themselves because that way you can try to make a way forward. But after you hear from outside, there is no more you can do. After I heard that, I told him that it's over, that same day. It's better for me to go where I will not see him. My parents didn't know I was dating him; there at my place you don't introduce a man until he is coming to pay dowry for you. I never even explained to my mother about the heartbreak because it's a shameful thing.

When I asked him about it, he never gave me a proper excuse. But by then I already had the proposal from my good friend – she's like a sister – to come to South Africa. So, you can say that it was the heartbreak that allowed me to go.

A NEW LIFE

My first choice was to go to Canada, but getting a visa for Canada is just, like, difficult. And it's also expensive apart from that. When my sister told me about South Africa, I just took Canada out of my mind. Now all that was ringing in my mind was South Africa, South Africa, South Africa!

But when I decided to leave home it was not so easy. My friends, my parents, everybody – it was like they are all going to miss me. But I didn't care if they were missing me because in my mind I knew I just want to go to South Africa! When I used to see it on TV, I thought it was just a place for whites. Whites and whites and whites. I didn't know that I could meet black people like me in South Africa. When I first landed, the people I was seeing were only black. Black! Then, after the airport I started seeing a few of the whites.

My sister and her husband were still here when I arrived, so they came to the airport and picked me up and took me to their place. They were staying in a flat in Sunnyside with her friend, Titilayo, who owned a hair salon. After a few months they moved to Angola, so I stayed there in the flat with Titilayo, and sometimes there were salon workers who would come to stay and pass the time with us while they were looking for another place to stay.

I started going with Titi to the salon every morning and watching the way they were working. That is where I learnt to do hair, even though dressing hair was never in my mind. But when I saw the way they were doing it I got more interest. I discovered that hair can make money so I put all my interest and my mind in it.

At Titilayo's salon I was only doing the parting on the hair, and then she would come braid. Titi didn't give me a chance to prove myself. I was not angry, I just needed to go somewhere where I could also work by myself, so I could show what I have been learning. I had to look for my independence, and I found another salon where I could work.

Here I am today, a professional on my own. I can do any hairstyle I want. As long as they show me the hairstyle I can do it. I do bonding, straight up, singles, whatever. I still work in Sunnyside; I rent a mirror at a salon here. We are mostly Nigerians working here, but our clientele is mixed. The South Africans don't treat me any different way, we are all just together, we work as a family, we work as a team. But you know there is no way you will be with someone and there are no misunderstandings; the most important thing is to keep to each other's rules. We all have our rules.

Today, if I go back to Nigeria I can stand on my own and show them that this is the work I learnt in South Africa and they will value my work a lot because I was trained in a first-class place. So I am not interested in teaching anymore, or going back to school. I am enjoying my work.

LOOKING FOR LOVE AND MARRIAGE

I dated a South African for three months when I first entered the country. But our dating was not like going to bed. My dream was to marry a South African. I wanted to marry a foreigner, someone different from my culture entirely. He was also a nice person – kind. But his church was different; they call his church the Zion Christian Church (ZCC). This kind of church is also in my country, and they are this kind of funny church. Women need to cover their hair and wear long skirts. They have too many rules and regulations.

I heard from other foreigners that South African men are not nice, that they don't take care of their wives, that they beat their wives, this and that. Me? I don't want any man that will beat me. But my boyfriend, he was a good person.

It's not that Nigerian men are different. All men are the same. But the truth is that, in anything, in marriage, you have to pray for your taste. What you want in marriage may be very different from what I want.

I won't lie to you, the ZCC guy, I really loved him, and he also loved me. He promised to pay my lobola in Nigeria and visit my place. We agreed. But the reason I washed my hands of him is one day came when I had to do my visa extension, because it was going to expire in one month and I wanted to get a permit for residence.

I said, 'Since we want to get married and you have rights to make me remain here, why don't you follow me to Home Affairs so you can assist me in having a permit to make me stay?' So he accepted. But the day that we were supposed to do that, he refused. He said his parents said he mustn't release any of those papers.

I said, 'But, ah! I thought you told your parents that you have a Nigerian you are wanting to marry, and they support you and are on with it?'

He was scared or – I don't really know – but later he regretted it. He called and was telling me he was sorry, we can still start afresh, he can give me those documents and everything. I told him it is too late. I felt so bad, so disappointed. That is when I saw that maybe the love is not true love.

Later I did my permit on my own. I found another person to do the papers with, to be my life partner. He is South African, he is the one I sign papers with for Home Affairs but he is not my real husband. My own husband is a Nigerian. This life partner is now a friend, a family friend. I even invited him yesterday for dinner. I was even making another plan to buy him a phone, clothes and everything he needs so I can send it off to him. He is part of us.

WHAT ELSE DOES A WOMAN WANT?

I married a Yoruba man from Nigeria. We met at the salon where I was working before. I think he is the one who first started monitoring me, seeing how I was, feeling like maybe I was the best for him. We used to work together at that salon – he used to do nails. So gradually, gradually, when we were waiting for customers, we would talk to each other. He used to ask about my tribe, about where I'm from and I would also ask him a little bit, too.

After he would close, he would come and wait for me, following me up and down. It used to get to be too much! People liked saying we were dating. But he was a Muslim and I didn't really like Muslims as I'm a Christian, and he was the type that had a long beard.

One day he asked me if I was single or married. So, I told him I was single. He said that his mother was pestering him to get married and that he would like to have me as his wife. I told him that I would go and think about it. From there he would still come to me. One day I told him, 'How can it work if we are from different religions?' He said it can still work: his father is Christian; his mother is Muslim. The boys follow their father, the two girls follow their mother. I only told my sister about this. My parents didn't know he was a Muslim until he paid my dowry.

There is something I told him, which is very, very difficult for him to do.

'Before we are having relationship, you will first of all cut all the beard. I can't walk with you with all these things that you have. I don't like all this beard, it makes you look dirty to me.'

He didn't say anything from there. After that day I went to work and didn't see him. Later he called me on the phone to see if I had already closed.

I told him, 'No, but why didn't you come today?'

He said, 'I am just having headache, but when you close I will come collect you.'

That day I was so busy. By the time I closed it was evening, and I'm a lady; I can't walk from town to Sunnyside alone so I called him. When I saw him I was shocked.

'You cut it?!'

It's a very big task to find someone who would do that for you, but he did it. That is when I knew he really loved me.

I didn't like him at first because I didn't want to marry into that tribe. But because he had the characters and qualities I wanted – well, that is why I didn't mind the culture. He doesn't drink or smoke and he doesn't womanise. He is quiet and doesn't have friends. What else does a woman want?

From there we started seeing each other and I became pregnant. I told him that in my place you don't get pregnant without someone paying your dowry. But I never saw him as someone who has even R5 000. He was staying in a shared space – he didn't even rent half of a room. He looked like someone who didn't have anything so I was pitying him.

But he said to me, 'Let's just arrange,' and said he will send his family to my place.

'For what? You don't have R100!'

Then he said to me he had R20 000! That is when he sent his people to my place, they did the introductions and everything for the wedding. I never told my family I was pregnant. It was only after one month, after doing that dowry, that I told my sister. I never told my mother because she is that type that has a free heart, she will be so happy and she will tell anyone; she will broadcast the news for you and you can never detect where your enemy is. She will say 'Oh! Thank God! I'm happy my daughter is pregnant.' And it's not everybody who can be happy for you. Immediately after I gave birth I told my mom. She was so happy she was crying tears of joy.

Getting married without my family was not so easy. But the truth is that it's what I wanted. And they must also want the same thing as me. The family I come from, my mom, mostly she wants my happiness in anything I do.

ON TRADITION

The traditions for getting married in Nigeria are very different from South Africa. The way I understand it, in South Africa, if you have the baby without doing the right thing, then you are going to pay damages. It is not that way in Nigeria.

The right thing to do in Nigeria is, if you are pregnant before marriage, you have to get married before you give birth. So Nigerians, they don't charge damages.

Even with lobola, there are some tribes that have very expensive lobola like in South Africa. But there are other tribes that are not like that. In some parts, lobola is just to buy a big basin of bread. But for an Igbo girl, our lobola is also expensive. Very, very expensive.

Our last-born, my youngest sister, is a nurse in Nigeria. She is also holding herself, trying to make sure that she doesn't get pregnant before she gets married. You know the disadvantage, the main problem there, is your parents will suffer, especially your mother. If your own child is pregnant before marriage, a mother will not come out and talk to the other women because they will talk too much shit. They will treat her so cheap and tell her so many things. She will even be crying every day.

Another thing, you must not make a mistake and have a baby when you live in the family home or have a baby that doesn't have a father. Nobody will marry you again. That is why your parents make sure they take care of you; they pamper you, they safeguard you until you're grown up and know what is good and right.

But if you fall pregnant when you are in your family home, your brothers or their wives, they will start insulting you, telling you all sorts of things, saying that you must go and marry and leave their home. You start receiving those insults. It can even make someone drink acid and die. That's why it's important to hold yourself very well and make sure that you get married.

Like me now, the way I have one daughter with my husband, if something makes us separate today and I go home, no one is going to marry me again. But in South Africa our Nigerian men are busy dying for a woman who has like five children with different fathers, so they know that back home what they are doing in our own country is not nice.

WHEN THEY DO XENOPHOBIA, THEY START WITH THE NIGERIANS

The remarks of Zulu king Goodwill Zwelithini in April 2015, in which he compared foreigners to lice and said they must leave the country, brought with it a violent upsurge of xenophobic attacks targeted at African immigrants throughout the country. The violence resulted in a number of deaths, the burning of bodies, the looting of shops owned by African immigrants and the displacement of a number of immigrants and locals.

The xenophobic attacks, sweetheart, it was so, so, so, so hot! My parents in Nigeria were calling us, asking us if there is a way for us to come back. They were calling us, saying that we must not go anywhere, that we mustn't go outside because once they see somebody from Nigeria they're gonna be killed. Our government in Nigeria was also trying to figure out a way to deal with this; they were going to charter flights for all of us who wanted to come back.

At that time we were all so scared. We were seeing from the news on TV that even some Nigerians were killed. For two days I stayed inside my flat. But after that, when I had a client, I would go out and do the work I needed to do and then I would go back home. I was so, so afraid.

My husband was still going to work. He never mentioned being scared, but he told me to be very careful and not to take the baby to crèche until everything calmed down. Those are the things that show me he is scared, but as a man he can't say it. But in Sunnyside there were not too many victims. There are a lot of foreigners here, people from all over, so it was safer here. We didn't experience it like people in the locations.

Going to the location to stay is very dangerous. Because during that time, they would go and steal and take away everything that belongs to the Nigerians. During that time of the xenophobia, most of the Nigerians in the locations – they kill them, take their money, take their home, take their shop, take everything they have. I became very afraid of people from South Africa then, but now I'm not scared anymore. Things are fine now.

If there are ten South Africans, let's just say six of them don't want us to be here. And I know the reasons because I have studied this xenophobia, this making war happen. When the South Africans do xenophobia, they start with the Nigerians. They are saying Nigerians take over everything. This is the annoying part of it. They never like us even for one day. They say Nigerian men steal their women. Those are most of their reasons. They make their women ask for money. Money, money, money! When a South African dates a Nigerian woman, she will never go for a South African again. She will just look for another Nigerian. Nigerian men look after their women very well. They can do everything for you; they help you to pay rent, buy food. It's not this thing of everything fifty-fifty like with South Africans.

But some of the South Africans, they have a good heart and want a good government. There are those who don't want this xenophobia and they really want peace. No matter what the xenophobia did to us, I still love South Africa and I still love to stay here. Even if I go back to Nigeria I can only go to visit. I'll come back to this South Africa.

There is no way my daughter will grow up in Nigeria. She was born here, and I would like her to grow up here. She will go home and visit but she'll live here. I don't think she will manage in another place and, besides, there are more opportunities here for her, even if she is a girl.

Except – if tomorrow I wake up from sleep and hear that the government says we should go back to our country, then you can see me leave this place and go back to Nigeria. Then from Nigeria I will go to another country.

9

THIS LAND IS OUR LAND

Lufuno Gogoro

AGE WHEN INTERVIEWED: 36
BORN: Ha Mailula, Venda, South Africa
INTERVIEWED IN: Freedom Park, Soweto, Johannesburg, South Africa
INTERVIEWED BY: Dudu Ndlovu
PHOTOGRAPHED BY: Oupa Nkosi

Lufuno Gogoro was born in a village in Venda – one of ten bantustans or 'black homelands' established by the apartheid government, and which now forms part of Limpopo province. In 1993, he left his grandmother to live in Johannesburg with his mother, who was a domestic worker. Along with his mother and other community members, they occupied land in Soweto that later would be known as Freedom Park. A community leader actively involved in many political movements and community projects, Gogoro served as the spokesperson for the Greater Gauteng Business Forum, an organisation made up of informal businesses that has called for the closure of small, foreign-owned shops operating in townships across the province.

Growing up in Venda, I did almost everything a rural kid would do. We had a mud house and you could see the poverty; it was there. You know, a simple thing like bread was very scarce, so you would only get to enjoy a loaf of bread once or twice a year. You would survive on pap and *morogo* and cabbage.

So you grow up without anything; we could not afford toys to play with. If you played soccer, you played with your bare feet as we could not afford soccer boots. I would even go to school barefoot during the winter. But back then we thought that was a normal life. Most of the things we experienced were things that other families experienced. We didn't care much about it then, but when you look back you realise a lot of things were a challenge.

In school, we didn't get treated the same as someone who was from a family that was better off. I remember my three best friends, we all shared the name Lufuno. They were not beaten or sent to the principal's office. But others like me, they were beaten and even made to do manual work like scrubbing the floors or watering the garden. It is what inspired me to become involved in community debates.

When I was in standard six, I realised that we were not being treated well by the teachers; sometimes they would just skip a class and sit outside. I organised a strike that lasted the whole week. Even though I was not actually aware of what I was doing, I was an activist from an early age.

I always valued education – maybe it's because I was raised with Christian values and I used to read the Bible a lot. I was inspired by David, who was a fighter. My grandmother forced me to go to church. You know, in this whole world if God should ask me who should I bring back from the dead, it is my grandmother. She was a loving person, a protective woman who was always there trying to provide for us. But it was difficult, very, very difficult. My grandmother needed to have a pass in order to move around her own country. A lot of things were happening, and now you realise that it was by the grace of God that we have arrived to where we are today.

But back then I didn't like church. It was only in 2004 that I found my church, the one I attend now. They were holding a crusade and I saw a girl; she promised to meet with me at the church service. I went to the service drunk, just to meet the girl, and was sobered up by the preacher. He was talking about the land and how God wanted us to have land here on earth and not just wait for heaven. I gave my life to Jesus that night and forgot to look for the girl I had gone to meet.

OCCUPYING THE LAND

In 1993, when I first came to Johannesburg to live with my mother, I was 13. Ever since then I have been based in Freedom Park.

During that time, the people of Soweto were identifying open land to occupy. I got into the mix of things, following my mother and other people of Soweto, actually starting to understand the struggle for land. When we first arrived, we prayed and others performed their rituals. Freedom Park was farmland with a lot of trees and snakes, but at the time it was earmarked for industrial development.

My mother was one of the community leaders leading people to occupy the land. When you see your parent, or a person close to you doing something, being in the frontline fighting against the police and soldiers, it just makes you want to be involved.

I didn't understand exactly what was happening because I was still very young. But looking back it is what got me interested in becoming more politically inclined. My mother used to address meetings and encourage people, especially other women, to take the lead because most men would be at work during the day. We would go to meetings and marches even though our parents would shout at us, saying we needed to remain at the back. But we always found a way to go there and see what was happening when they were fighting, throwing stones and ducking rubber bullets. I think my mother had a silent prayer to say 'God, may you protect my kids,' because everyone, older people, middle-aged people, children, all of us were fighting. As kids we didn't understand the gravity of the situation and how dangerous it was to fight the security people. We were just following, unaware of the danger even though there would be hippos [armoured vehicles] surrounding us, just like in Marikana.

Every day was a struggle, but there was unity among different ethnic groups, coming together fighting for a common cause. They were all saying, 'We want our land, we want to have a place to stay, we cannot continue to pay rentals for backyards.'

It was exciting having to duck rubber bullets – a tiny boy picking up stones and fighting with the police; sometimes making up some ground where you can play soccer; meeting different groups who speak a different language to yours. It was interesting. I think it's one of the times I cherish because it gave me a way to understand people who are united in terms of a purpose or a common goal. When they come together they can achieve that, despite where they come from.

WE WANTED FREEDOM PARK TO BECOME A TOWNSHIP

When we first settled here, there were no shacks, no proper stands. To say 'We are here,' we made plastic houses so that we could have a roof over our heads. We were fortunate that we were never evicted.

In 1994, before the first democratic elections, Freedom Park was declared a community by the African National Congress (ANC) and the previous government, which was led by FW de Klerk. I was fortunate to be around when the ANC leaders, led by Tokyo Sexwale, came and told us that they had started preparation for cutting stands. I think it was a blessing that the ANC understood the need for people to have a place to stay. They negotiated with the then-government to say, 'You cannot remove people from this land; allow them to stay.'

But it was still just an informal settlement. The government needed to support it. They needed to supply mobile toilets and pipes to transport clean and drinkable water to communal taps close to where the people are living. So it was not to say that, okay, now because the ANC says you cannot be moved, automatically we were going to get things. It was still a challenge.

Freedom Park was actually made up of private land owned by the Golden Triangle Development Company and land that belonged to the Roman Catholic Church. The church said people could build there, so the municipality said people couldn't be removed from that land. The private land, where the owners were white – well, that was where they said we needed to be moved from – and that was the part where I was staying.

By 1996, I was 16 and part of the leadership and it was then that we had to meet with the so-called landowners. I remember there was a man called Winston Smith, and others whose names I have forgotten, who said, 'This is our land and we want people to be moved out.'

That nearly happened, because in 1999 there was a big meeting where the municipality leaders announced that we were going to be moved to Vlakfontein, which is about four to eight kilometres from Freedom Park. We had to start mobilising ourselves to fight. The government sent Vukani Security, the Red Ants, to remove us in 1999. We had to physically fight against them; some lost their eyes, other people were crippled in other ways, and others died. It was a war.

That's when we joined an organisation called the Landless People's Movement, which was fighting against forced removal in informal settlements. We were fighting to remain there, fighting to say there must be proper community development: housing, schools, toilets and water, playing grounds and shops.

Eventually a community meeting was called to say that no one was going to be moved. The government bought some of the land from the white people and a week later we were called to a meeting where the local municipality managers came with a map and plans to show us how the community would look. That is what we wanted. We wanted a proper settlement. We wanted Freedom Park to become a township.

In 1997, the show house – a 45-square-metre building – was constructed. We wanted people to see that this was our destiny. The housing plan was developed and people were encouraged to put together their R20 or R30 to build this show house. It has remained as it is up until today, as a place for community meetings and projects.

In 2001, the municipality started the process of registration. They said only 3 000 families were going to be allocated stands but there were about 7 000 families who needed them. But we wouldn't allow for those 4 000 families to be moved. Eventually the government ended up agreeing that they could occupy the open spaces.

Allocation of stands started in 2002, but Johannesburg city officials were also biased toward the ANC. They were always isolating those who didn't belong to the party. There was a lot of corruption and maladministration in the housing allocation. Some people who were never part of Freedom Park were brought in from the outside and given stands. So, it was a mess; things were not okay.

At the time I belonged to an opposition party – the Socialist Party of Azania – and we were always at loggerheads with the ANC. This party believes that the end of apartheid did not truly liberate black people in South Africa but that the ANC sold out to white capital. We were always protesting, closing down the street, even marching to the house of the former mayor, Amos Masondo, voicing our anger and dissatisfaction.

FREEDOM IS ECONOMIC TRANSFORMATION AND THE RETURN OF THE LAND

In 2004, I was recruited by the ANC Youth League, though I never really liked the ANC. My political background is black consciousness and pan-Africanism. I was inspired by Steve Biko, Robert Sobukwe, Thomas Sankara and Robert Mugabe. African leaders who were saying Africa belongs to Africans; those who were talking about the land and the economy. They were saying, 'If you want to have proper freedom, it has to come with economic transformation and the return of the land.'

I was raised within the political framework to know that whites are thieves. They have stolen our land. It cannot belong to them, and it has to be returned to us, on our terms and conditions, so we can redistribute it to suit the mainly black majority, who have been isolated and subjected to landlessness. When we are happy, then we can say the whites can continue to use the remaining land.

In addition to the Youth League, I was also involved with the Soweto Electricity Crisis Committee, who were dealing with problems of electricity and water. We said water should be free and that those who are able must pay but those who cannot must not, and they must have water. We had the Operation Khanyisa movement where if you were unable to pay for electricity and the municipality switched you off, they would go and reconnect it. There was the Anti-Privatisation Forum, which was taking on mainstream political issues like the privatisation of Eskom, Telkom and the railways and mines, because this was adding to retrenchments and unemployment. When the Democratic Left Front was formed, I was part of those people, too. And when the ANC wanted to pass the Secrecy Bill, so that we wouldn't be able to access government information, I was part of the Right to Know campaign.

It was in 2011 that the Youth League finally took a decision to say we were going to fight for the land and for nationalisation. Even before the ANC expelled Julius Malema from the Youth League for raising issues like this, we had already formed the Economic Freedom Fighters, because land expropriation without compensation and nationalisation was not being raised within the ANC; those who were raising it were being expelled.

THE GREATER GAUTENG BUSINESS FORUM

The Greater Gauteng Business Forum (GGBF) was formed in 2011 by local traders who felt businesses owned by foreigners were illegal and who threatened 'drastic measures', including violent protests, if its demands for the closure of those businesses were not met. Gogoro was the group's spokesperson at the time.

The GGBF is an umbrella body which brought together different small business forums across Gauteng to help solve problems faced by tuckshop owners in the townships. It planned for bookkeeping training, as well as assistance with regulating tuckshops and other small businesses. But we also wanted to help interpret the Immigration Act and come up with a moratorium on how to stop the influx of people, how to integrate those who are already here, to form a working relationship so the foreign tuckshop owners could teach us how to do business, and to report illegal activities.

For example, we used to raid the foreign-owned shops and found one shop in Orlando with a fridge that had human body parts in it. Some of these shop owners used to fight each other and they would use the local youth as hit men.

In 2012, the violence against foreigners broke out again because some youth in Katlehong tried to rob a foreign-owned tuckshop, and one of the boys was killed. In response, the community attacked the tuckshop owner and the violence spread across different townships, with people looting tuckshops and chasing the foreign owners out of their communities. Because the GGBF already had structures in place in different locations, we could respond to the violence by asking the foreigners to leave. We said we could not protect foreigners over the local people, so we wanted the government to see to it that the foreigners left.

At the time of the attacks, I was a researcher for the Social Change Research Unit at the University of Johannesburg, helping to document protests in informal settlements, so I was close to the issue. It was this: people are unemployed and these others are just coming to take over *spaza* shops everywhere and buying the locals out. It was becoming a problem and nobody was saying anything. That is when we started to want to understand what is actually the problem. Instead, people started to fight.

People were fighting against Pakistanis, Ethiopians and Somalians. Through lack of political consciousness, it became a situation where the Zulus started to say, 'This is our land and everyone else can just go.' They started to attack the Zimbabweans and those who came from Mozambique, who we have lived with for so many years. As long as you could not speak proper Zulu, you became a target. The Tsongas from Limpopo – they were set alight. The Venda were also subjected to attacks. We had to go out as leaders from different places to say, 'Let's come together so that we can prevent violence,' and also to look at how we resolve and stop the influx of foreigners coming to take over the *spaza* shops and other small economic sectors so that we can put bread on the table. We were saying local people must be a priority no matter what.

If you go to Botswana and start a business there, you are given a period to operate. You cannot operate without a local partner. It is happening everywhere – in Zimbabwe and other African countries. If you are a foreigner, you are not even allowed to operate a business unless you invest. So why is it that in South Africa when you raise this it becomes xenophobia?

There has been this notion to say that foreigners – like Mozambicans and Zimbabweans – are cheap, so they don't mind being paid less money. To us it was a problem. You cannot subject people who are coming here to work, who have families, to low salaries because they are foreigners. Unfortunately people never understood our ideas, what we wanted to do. They just said we are xenophobic, but we were asking the foreigners to leave, to stop the violence and put South Africans first.

In every community struggle there are elements of criminal activity. There are those who see the opportunity to commit crime, and you cannot prevent that. Everyone wants to be settled, wants to have a proper job, wants to have proper businesses to be able to afford the basic needs. If you can't, what do you do? You resort to crime, target the foreign nationals, and influence other people, who are not even aware of your intention – and that is where this thing became xenophobic.

SOUTH AFRICA IS NOT ENOUGH FOR ALL OF US

But in South Africa there has never been xenophobia. It is Afrophobia. We are saying as Africans we don't like ourselves, we are fighting against ourselves. So if we were also attacking white people, then it would become xenophobia. You cannot say it's xenophobia when you are attacking your own brothers.

My problem is when South Africa becomes a haven to criminals who pretend to be asylum seekers, only to find that they want to commit crimes at the expense of those who actually need asylum, protection and security.

You cannot run away from Zimbabwe because Robert Mugabe is brutal. People must unite. As South Africans we defeated apartheid. If a regime is a problem to the people, there is always an opportunity to defeat that regime because you mobilise people, you come together and you fight that regime. That doesn't amount to me being xenophobic. I just speak my mind. I don't support violence against non-South Africans, I don't support violence against anyone, but we also need to look at the issues. We cannot continue to have people who are running away from their countries because South Africa is not enough for all of us. South Africa must become a hope that influences democracy in other countries.

When the xenophobic violence broke out in 2008, there were no signs that this was going to happen. That thing spread all over. An outbreak can still happen, and this time when it happens nobody is going to stop it. People are going to die, because after we contained the situation, we never went back to say, 'Let's deal with this.'

Do you think by just saying, 'Stop the xenophobic attacks, we must love our African brothers,' that is enough? We will tell you, 'Okay sharp.' Then tomorrow I'm unemployed, start doing drugs and start to influence my friends to say, 'Let's go to that shop.' Then I go and break in and that particular foreigner maybe shoots at us and somebody dies there. Then the community comes and attacks.

The root cause of this problem is not a *spaza* shop, as such; this is a war that the government needs to deal with. This is a war which is being instigated by the world cartel, people who want to have control over the country's resources. Most of these *spaza* shops are just a front. The issue is they want to take over the land. These shops that you see everywhere, particularly in South Africa, they are not here because these people want to take bread. They are here because these people want to take our land. The Muslims want to occupy almost everywhere in the world and South Africa is up for grabs.

We need to think of the future of this country. We must never hate those who come to the country because they want asylum but we must never agree that everybody can just come and do what they want. If you are an asylum seeker, obviously you want security, you need to be fed but you are not here as an economic migrant, you cannot operate a business. You are not here to study, you are here because you are seeking asylum.

Why do you have the Pakistanis, Bangladeshis and Ethiopians coming to South Africa? You ask them, 'Why don't you want to go?' And they tell you, 'If we go back home they are going to kill us because we are here on a mission. We need to make sure that we make kids here.' After 20 years those kids will say, 'We are South Africans, this is our land, we were born here and we want to participate in politics.' If that happens, I'm telling you they are going to take over. We are going to have a situation of Israel and Palestine. The war continues.

Islam is an angry religion. It is a religion based on revenge and isolation. I do not have a problem personally with Islam. But I have a problem when it becomes a religion that murders and subjects women and children to abuse. There is no freedom of expression, of association or religion.

I'm not going to defend Christianity because there are those who are killing people in the name of Christianity. In our church, we believe that Christ came here on earth to address the covenant and government issues. When the government is failing the people, the church must correct government. Our people are being subjected to poverty and suffering because of politics and politicians. The church, as the core defender of the people, must speak.

When I go to church I don't pray that God will forgive my sins so that when I die I go to heaven and live. I ask God to give me strength to be able to do something different because I don't live in heaven, I live here on earth and there are challenges here. We are talking about the land, and the land is the economy, the land is wealth. I'm not going to wait until I die and go to heaven to have a rest.

10

ALIEN

Esther Khumalo

AGE WHEN INTERVIEWED: 41
BORN: Bulawayo, Zimbabwe
INTERVIEWED IN: Tembisa, South Africa
INTERVIEWED BY: Greta Schuler
PHOTOGRAPHED BY: Madelene Cronje

Esther Khumalo grew up in Zimbabwe with a Malawian father, who always reminded her that her ancestral home was in another country. She was married with two children when her husband decided to leave Zimbabwe to seek work in South Africa. Without official identification documents from either country, she travelled to Johannesburg when she was 21. After difficulties with her husband, she became a sex worker and, for more than a decade, has been crossing the border and engaging in sex work to earn money to care for her five children.

I don't have a passport because my father is from Malawi. I have a Zimbabwean ID, but I'm not a Zimbabwean citizen and I'm not a Malawian citizen. It's like I'm in between. I was born in Zimbabwe, but they say I'm not a citizen because my father is from Malawi. So, I have to apply for citizenship so that I can apply for a passport. Now, my ID's written 'alien'. I have to apply for citizenship so that they will cancel that 'alien'. I still ask myself: why am I an alien if I was born in Zimbabwe?

We were staying in a location in Bulawayo in a three-roomed house, painted green inside and out. We were a big family – 11 kids. Girls: we were sleeping in the sitting room; boys: they were sleeping in the kitchen. My father was a hard worker. Most of the time his money was paying school fees and feeding us. I remember every month he would buy groceries for a month – not a week. Even my mom used to be a hard worker. My uncle, a builder, was the one who was supposed to plaster inside the house. He got cross with my mom. She says, 'You're my brother, but you charge me too much! I won't pay you! I'll do it myself.' She took cement and plastered! Serious!

She was very strict. When you are from school, the gate was normally closed at six o'clock. After six, no one is going outside. My mom doesn't like daughters who go out and come back late. I started soccer when I was 14 years. Normally, I was going to play after school, so obviously I will come late. She said, 'You see, you run away from doing inside jobs to play soccer!' She hit me.

When I'm from school, I hide my short and maybe a T-shirt, everything in a Checkers, a plastic bag. I hide it in the branches near the gate. My mother used to sit on a sofa by the door, so she can see when you're going outside. 'Where are you going?' I would just say, 'I'm playing.' And then I would take my Checkers and run away and go and play soccer.

You see when you are a teenager, especially when you are a girl, your parents are strict because you can get pregnant. They wanted me to stay in the house. But after my father saw me playing soccer, he said, 'Wow, my daughter!'

I didn't see him outside but he's the one who saw me. By the time I go back home, he said, 'That's my good girl! I saw you playing! You scored a goal!' And then my father started to buy me boots, T-shirts, bags, for training. But my mother was very, very strict. My coaches used to go and beg Mom, 'We've got a big game, so please let Esther play. She's a good player.' And then my mom said, 'Okay, take my daughter but you must bring her back!'

I was playing for Ingwebu Breweries. They didn't pay us. They just said, 'Thanks, thanks, thanks.' It was 1991. Soccer was not like these days. Now all the people know soccer for ladies, but long time ago it was very difficult.

The coach, he was a soldier before. He used to train us hard: how to kick, how to chase, how to hit, everything from the start. I didn't know anything.

After some years, I change my team and go and play for Highlanders, which is a very big team. When we go out, like, to games in Botswana, they give us money to buy something to spoil us. Like, maybe we go to play in Botswana and they give us 100 pula, and then we buy some cosmetics, so when we go home we're carrying some Checkers. They see we're from outside the border.

By the time I was 16, I dropped school, but still I was playing for Highlanders. My mom is the one who made me drop school; she was complaining that I'll end up not studying because of soccer.

My mother said, 'I won't be paying for your school fees. I'll pay for your younger brother because the money is not enough.' And then I got angry. I started to change.

I said, 'Okay, you don't want to pay my school fees? Okay, it's fine.' And then I started to change. If she said, 'Wash those plates,' I say, 'No, I won't wash those plates. You didn't pay school fees for me so that I'd be here to wash these plates?'

ALL OF YOU, STRIP

That's when I fell in love with my first husband. When we're playing soccer, he comes and watches us. We get close, and then I get pregnant. I was still young, 17 years. My parents were very angry at me: 'See now you're pregnant because of this football.' I said, 'No, it's not football. I'm pregnant, but don't blame soccer for what I did.' My husband paid damages because I was very young. You know Africa, you have a baby when you are still at school or young and they pay damages because you are still young. So, I go back and stay with my first love and his parents. He was older than me, five years. He was not working, but he was playing soccer also.

I had my first-born in 1993. It's a boy. Maybe after my son was six months, I go back to play soccer again because I like soccer very, very much. Coming from my mother-in-law's house, I don't need money for transport. Just five minutes, I'm in the stadium. I leave my son with his aunties and go and play. If the baby is crying, you find my auntie coming, carrying the baby, saying, 'The baby is crying!' And then coach say, 'Go feed the baby!' And then I breastfeed the baby.

My husband was playing for another team and sometimes they would take him for temporary work. But by the time I have two babies, life was very hard. He said, 'I am not managing.' So, he decided to come to South Africa in 1996. He started working as a security guard for a clothes shop in Johannesburg.

Then I started visiting my husband. I left my kids in Zim with their grandmother and grandfather. I didn't use a passport. I jumped the border.

You'll meet someone there at Beit Bridge who knows the river and then they'll take us to the Limpopo River. When we're there at the Limpopo River, they say, 'All of you, strip.' You'll remain with panties or tights. Then you take your jean and put it here, on your neck, because you're going to wear it when you jump in the river. You jump the Limpopo, go with feet, and then the car will find you after the border. It's too expensive. By the time I started to come to South Africa, it was R700, but now it is R1 500. It's not bad because now R1 500 is nothing when you want to come to South Africa. Why I say it's nothing: people are hungry to come here to look for money. You see R1 500 is a lot of money, I don't want to lie, but when you start working you see this is nothing.

I would come to South Africa for six months, maybe a year, but when I come in 1997, I stay two years. I was just sitting, and my husband said, 'The whole day you are sitting, go and look for a job.'

By that time I didn't have a passport, but my friend who was staying in the same flat was a South African. She felt pity for me. She said, 'Here is my photocopy of my ID; go and look for a job.' One day I was very lucky. I saw a sign: 'Looking for a lady for a job.' They interviewed 16 of us, but two of us get jobs. So I was very lucky. First day I get job, there was overtime. So I went home late. Even when I go home, I was very happy. 'I'm now working!' I didn't care what kind of a job. This shop, where they were selling clothes, was right in town. I called to customers outside, 'Come in, come in! They are selling clothes very cheap!' It was very good.

A PRISON FOR FOREIGNERS

Then one day, I was maybe six months working there, I was arrested because I don't have papers. They take us to Lindela. When you enter Lindela, they ask: 'Who's got passport? ID? Asylum?' If you've got those things, you remain on the other side. It's like a prison of foreigners. It's big rooms with single beds. The guards come and count us to check us at night. In the morning, they come and count us again. There's a teatime – porridge and bread and tea – and then in the afternoon there is lunch. Then at night there is also a supper. But that food is not healthy. It's a dirty food, I don't want to lie. The way they cook it – maybe it's because they are cooking it for too much people. They allow visitors, and the visitors come and give you money. If you don't want to eat there, you go and buy in the shops. Because that food – the soup is like water. Of course, if you don't have someone to see you, you have to eat to survive.

My husband was the one who came to see me. He gave me a towel, Colgate, soap, everything. He gave me money: 'There's money. Maybe you go out and come back with this money. Sometimes these policemen will say, when you are going home, "Do you have money?"' And that's what happened.

I stayed there maybe for two weeks. By the time the guards were taking us to the cars for deportation, they were saying, 'Do you have money? Come this side.' So we made another queue, because I had money. I was carrying R600 – that was a lot of money by that time – but I hid it. I put separate: R300 this side, R300 this side. My husband had said, 'Don't give them all the money because you don't know what's going to happen.' Then we were nearly in Joburg; they came and opened the door. 'Who's got R500?' Someone who got R500 will pay, but me – I didn't pay because my husband told me they'll end up going down.

And then, I was maybe in Sophiatown and they said, 'So you have the money. How much do you have?' I think there were four of us. I said, 'Me, I've got R300.' Another said, 'I've got R350.' Another said, 'I've got R300.' You see? He ended up collecting that money. Then he opened the door of the car. He said, 'When I go inside, then you run away.' He didn't want people to see. And then he opened, and one by one we go. We stopped the taxis going to Joburg. And then I call my husband: 'I'm home.'

HOW TO DRESS LIKE A SOUTH AFRICAN

We foreigners used to run away because we didn't want police to arrest us. When police arrest you, you're going to lose the job because you're going to stay in Lindela for a long time. And you don't have a job anymore.

I still watch out for police. But now it's hard for them to identify me because I'm clever. I know how to dress so that people will not say this one is from Zim, this one is a foreigner. I know how to dress like a South African now.

South Africans dress different. When you come from home, you don't have trousers and tackies; you wear long dresses. You don't know the fashion of South Africa. You are scared when you're walking. Now, I'm not scared. I can walk and come upon the police and I don't care because I'm used to South African life. I don't run away. I just check: okay, on that corner there are police, and I just divert the route, but I don't show them. Others, when they see police, they start panicking.

Most of the time when they arrest they don't wear uniforms, they just put their civilian clothes. You see, I'm staying in Joburg for a long time. I know them. When you are in town, normally you can't stand in the corner, so usually when you see people standing, you start suspecting. What's going on there? And then if you check nicely, you can see from afar that they are pulling people, showing them cards. You have to be clever. I learnt when I started working as a sex worker, because I was staying with South Africans.

AFTER A WEEK I KNEW EVERYTHING

In 1999, my husband said, 'It's long time, you must go see the kids. You must go home.' Even me, I was complaining; I want to see my kids. He buy groceries, give me money, and then I go home. But in 2000, I came back. I knew where my husband was selling tomatoes, fruits, what-what. So I went there to the stand. Ha! He was shocked.

'You're here!'

'Yes, I'm here.' I thought maybe he would take me – where? To the flat. But he didn't.

He say to me, 'No, I can't take you where I'm staying. I'm staying with too much guys now. Since you left, things are different now. Don't worry, I will take you to your auntie.' I say my 'auntie' because my sister was married to her brother. I was wondering where my husband's going to take me. But when I reached the hotel, I was so shocked: it was full of people wearing miniskirts. I couldn't even look at them like this. My auntie came: 'Hello, hello, hello,' and greet us like this.

My husband said, 'There's your friend.' And then I was there in Diplomat Hotel, and my husband said to my auntie, 'There's Esther. If she doesn't know how to play soccer, teach her.'

Just like that. He leaves me, just like that. My auntie didn't want people to hear what was happening. She said 'Okay, let's go upstairs.' She took me through security and upstairs to her room. I stayed there nearly a week. She was paying rent. By that time, they used to share their rooms – two, two, two. So when she is working, I go to the toilet. Now I can see what is happening. Because every time when she comes, she tells me, 'Go outside to the passage.' After one week, she came with other girls; they were South African girls.

They said, 'You are abusing your auntie now. Your auntie is paying double rent. You are sitting here just eating. Your auntie's working; you also must work. There is a skirt.' It was very short – like this. 'Look how beautiful you are.'

And I was very young and beautiful. I said, 'No, no, I can't wear that skirt.'

They said, 'You can, because you have to pay rent. Who's going to do that for you?'

First day, I was just hiding my eyes, facing down. But the customers can see this one is new. They say, 'Come, let's go.' My auntie's friends say, 'Go, go with the customers.' They teach me to use condoms, what-what. First time I go, they follow because I don't know this job, and maybe the customer will take advantage of me. My auntie followed, too; she was outside with her friends. Then after ten minutes – because the customer thinking this one she's new she doesn't know the rules – they said, 'No, no, no!' They started knocking the door. 'Time up! Don't take advantage of this girl! Time up! Go!' Even me, I was starting to jump.

That guy say, 'Okay, I'll put another money.'

'Fine, if you put another money, it's okay. We'll wait outside. Put another money!' I was so surprised. 'Take the money!'

You see, I didn't know. But after a week, I knew everything.

PAY THE RENT, SUPPORT THE KIDS, SUPPORT HIM AND ALSO ME

I stayed at the hotel for so long. I started to have a lot of money. When I visited home in 2006, I met this guy. I just fell in love with him. He said, 'Me, I will also go to South Africa.' I said, 'That's fine. I will meet there.' Maybe in three months' time, he to South Africa. We started dating. I wasn't working the way I used to work because I was in love for a long time. And then I get pregnant.

I was very lucky with the people I was staying with. My best friend was a Tswana, Lebo. Lebo's like a shortcut name. Before I was eight months, she said to me, 'Here in South Africa it's very hard. Since you are pregnant and you don't have papers, take this. Say you lost your ID.' It's like that paper waiting for ID. She said, 'Take this paper to the hospital; they will book you. Just tell them, "I lost my ID, and I applied for another one".' So I book there in Johannesburg Hospital with Lebo's ID. My third-born is registered as Lebo's daughter, not mine.

After that, I stayed at home, not working. After maybe one year or so, life started to change. See, when you're not working, things are different. If you don't have money, things are hard. And then I started to argue with my husband. He'd fight unnecessary things with me. He used to hit me. When he was drunk, he used to come home and collect the money, then go with the girlfriend. That's when I said let me go back to my old job.

It was very hard for me to tell him what I was doing. I used to say, 'I'm a shoplifter. I go to Durban or to Cape Town.' I just lie. I would go to a hotel in Pretoria for maybe Thursday, Friday, Saturday, Sunday, and then I go home. His mom is the one who would take care of the baby.

We stayed there in Yeoville. My husband used to drink and go to work sometimes. Or he doesn't go to work. His job finished. So I'm the only one now who's working. Pay the rent. Support the kids. Support him, and also me. To me it was very hard because I had to support those ones at home and this one in South Africa.

WE KNOW YOU, ZIMBABWEANS. YOU USE MUTI

I was working as a sex worker then in the street. We work there, but it's not 100 per cent safe. Because sometimes, the customers they're not good. In the street, there's always challenges, especially on the corners. In the street, you know each other. These girls are from Zimbabwe and these are South African. On the corners, there's a group of South Africans and a group of Zimbabweans. Sometimes if you go where there's South Africans, they can chase you. 'You Zimbabweans, go, go that side, because here we don't want Zimbabweans! You're using muti, and I'm not getting enough money because of you!'

I end up saying, 'No, no. This street, no one belongs to this street. This is a street. All of us, we come here to look for money for our kids. So there's no one who will chase me here. I will stand here. Unless if you come and fight me, I won't go anywhere, because I'm here to look for money. I won't go anywhere.' That's what I told them, and then they said, 'Why this girl, she's like this?' And then they check my face, and I was serious. Maybe they end up scared because I managed to stand up for myself.

And then, after some days, I take Nobuhle – we're like sisters – and Nobuhle was just standing next to me. I told her don't go to that corner because they will chase you. Just stand next to me. Then they just started talking, but they didn't come to us.

'You see now, she brings another one!'

I said to Nobuhle, 'Just be quiet. Keep on working.'

And then they didn't come back again and say, 'You bring another lady, what-what, you must go.'

No, because they were not sure about me. This one managed to stand up for herself. Maybe she can fight us.

One week, it was cold; we make fire for us, only me and Nobuhle. And the other corner, just small distance, they make their own fire because you can't sit together. South African girls say, 'We know you, Zimbabweans. You use muti. If you are here, we won't make any cents here because of you.'

Most of the times, clients like Zimbabwean ladies. That's why South African ladies sometimes get angry with us. You see, because they say most of the time when they're complaining with South Africans, they say, 'You Zimbabwean ladies, when you're sleeping with the clients, you do like this – you're active. So why are you doing that because these people are clients?' So normally, we fight with those things. That's the problem. And then the clients, they say, 'You South Africans, you don't know how to take care of a man.' That's why we end up not liking each other: because of that.

But after some time, maybe two to three weeks, there's South African ladies in the corner. That day, it was only two. And then one of the South Africans finds a 'whole night' and then there remained one South African. So that one was scared. And we are two here. And then we didn't have enough wood for the fire. And she say, 'Come, come, let's make fire one place, you see, because I'm alone here, I'm scared.' Where we are, there is too much wind. We go there; we sit with her. And then we started talking.

'Hey, don't worry! Some of my friends are jealous. They say you are making too much money.' She told us that. 'See, here, we are working, all of us. Even you, you are working. It's not that we are working only. This place is busy. We all get enough money.'

We end up getting used to each other, because at night it's not safe – on our corner it was very quiet and dangerous at night. Some guys come to provoke us or to steal, so if we are close to each other, it is better.

MY BAD DAY

In the street, we must be strong. If you find someone who's harsh, and he discovers that you are a foreigner, he takes advantage of that. He knows you won't go to the police. South Africans are different. If you are South African and you are a sex worker, you've got that power.

In 2012, I was in the street. And then I see this car kept on passing, passing, and then he stopped. I go there, 'Hello! How are you?'

He said, 'I want business.'

'R50.'

We were doing business here but he said he doesn't want to leave his car. And then I said, 'Okay, fine, let's go to a car wash – you go in and then you do it in the car.' He said, 'No. I don't want to do dirty stuff in my car. Let's go to my house.' You see, I trusted that man. I said, 'Let's go.' He said he's staying in Rosettenville. On the way there, he asked if I was hungry, and I say, 'Yes.' He went and buy KFC for me. I started to relax. This person is good; he's buying food for me. I thought maybe I would end up spending the whole night, and he would pay me nice money.

We went to a building. He drive the car into the building and just park there. He said, 'Come out.' By the time I come out, I noticed this building. They didn't plaster it. It was still dirty. There were papers; there were plants inside. I said, 'Where are we?' He just keep on quiet like he didn't hear me. I say, 'Are you staying here?'

He said, 'Shut up.' He started to change now, you see. And then I just check: there's no house here. If someone's doing bad things, you say today is my bad day. What those other girls told me now is happening to me. Today is my bad day. I was just speaking in my heart. It didn't come out: 'Oh God, please protect me.' It's like I was praying inside: 'Oh God, please protect me. I love my kids.'

'Come here!' He was in a room, but there was no floor. They were still renovating that room. He said to me, 'Bend, bend, bend!' I said, 'Here's a condom.' 'Shut up!' He fuck me without a condom. And then after that he say, 'Bitch!' He push me, and drive off.

I was wearing a panty and trying to wipe myself. The car gone – zoom. Leave me in that abandoned building. I was very scared to come out. I just said in my heart, 'Thank God he didn't kill me.' When I go outside, I run. I run as if maybe he's following me, but he isn't following me. I run, I run, I run, I run, I run.

In the morning, that's when I went to Esselen Clinic. That's where they gave me the tablets. I didn't go to the road for some days, because I was still in shock. Sometimes other girls, they tell us stories, but that day it happened to me. I didn't go to the police. Because why? What am I going to do? What must I say? If it happens to South African girls, they can take the case to the police. It's better because the South African can manage to go there to the police camp and put a case. But we foreigners, we are scared even to go to the police camp because we don't have papers. It's not me alone. Even other girls, foreigners, I don't think they've reported their case to the police.

So I just drank my tablets, and then I go back to work again. After times goes, I started to forget a little bit, a little bit. Sometimes you got clients, too much, and money and then I'm happy. That thing, that bad thing, I started to forget a little bit by bit.

WARD 21

The first time I went to go and test, I was not feeling well. I was vomiting and had a headache. If you're sick, you have to test for HIV first before you attend to the doctor at General. And then after a week, I went to go and collect my results for CD4 count, and that's when my CD4 count was 297. Then they tell me, 'You must go to Ward 21.' They won't explain too much about your sickness because in Ward 21 they're going to do that in the classes. I started treatment. If you start the treatment, you go through the doctor. They don't just give you the treatment. There are queues for doctors. That's where I told the doctor, I'm not feeling well. That's when I took the pregnancy test. That's when I found out that I'm pregnant. The doctor said, 'That's why you're not feeling okay. But there's no problem if you are pregnant as long as you drink your tablets nicely.'

After that, the doctor said to me, 'Since you are pregnant, I can't keep you here in Ward 21. I will send you back to General Hospital so that you'll book for the pregnancy, and they'll make you a file so you'll continue taking ARVs.'

MY NAME IS OWETHU DLAMINI

Since I lost my asylum, I lost everything. You see, I opened a bank account with my asylum. And now, I'm just stranded. I don't have asylum. I don't have a passport. It's just me. That's why it was hard for me, even when I was with my fourth child, to carry on with my treatment. Because when they are opening another file, they say I don't have asylum. I give them this photocopy. They say, 'No, we want an asylum. This one is expired.' That's why I stopping getting my treatment, because of these papers. They refused.

I was angry. I stayed maybe a year without my treatment. I was thinking, what if I go to Esselen Clinic, they will say they want papers again. I went to Esselen. I opened a new file. I didn't write my name. I wrote the wife of my brother's name, Owethu Dlamini. I change everything. My name is Owethu Dlamini. Even now I have a file called Owethu Dlamini. Even now I'm lying about my identity because I want the treatment. I can't survive without my treatment, you see. And then I moved to Pretoria. In Esselen Clinic that's where they wrote a transfer letter here in Mayibuye Clinic. And then in Mayibuye Clinic, they don't call me Esther, they call me Owethu Dlamini, because I want what? To get treatment. Unfortunately, I was pregnant again.

My baby was born here. She's five months now. Why should they not give her the access for South African citizenship? I've heard some people talking that there's a process. Birth record and health card, you can go home to Zimbabwe and apply for the papers, but there's a fine because you didn't get the baby that side. All I know is that the paper is written 'alien' also, because it's not from Zimbabwe, it's from South Africa. What I know, if you are not born in Zimbabwe, you do not have that citizenship in Zimbabwe. Their birth certificate is going to be written 'alien' because they were born here in South Africa. Even if I have money, if I have a hundred dollars, and I go to Zimbabwe to take my baby's birth certificate, it's going to be written 'alien'.

I WANT TO GO HOME FOREVER

You see, my story's very painful. But I love my kids. Three of my babies were born here in South Africa. It's my home now. I'm from Zimbabwe by birth but my home is Malawi because my father is from Malawi. My parents are staying in Malawi now, they moved from Bulawayo. Growing up, my father used to tell us, one day, you want to know where you come from. And then he used to tell us: your home is Malawi, my village. He used to tell us that like a story. When they go to Malawi, they used to write us some letters, and I just keep that address in my mind. When I started working as a sex worker, I have too much money, and then I want to go and see my parents. It was 2010. I surprised them. Even my mother cried. My father was very shocked to see me. How many kilometres, I didn't know, but I was there with my parents.

I was there in Malawi but I didn't use my documents since I don't have a passport. I don't want to lie, I used Nobuhle's passport. You see Nobuhle and me, we look alike. So I used Nobuhle's passport to get to Malawi to see my parents. In Zimbabwe, where I was born, I'm an alien. But when I want to go to Malawi again, I will go to the embassy and tell them I want to go home forever so they will give me that letter to go forever.

11

ONE DAY IS ONE DAY

Alphonse Nahimana

AGE WHEN INTERVIEWED: **49**
BORN: Butare, Rwanda
INTERVIEWED IN: Braamfontein, Johannesburg, South Africa
INTERVIEWED BY: Suzy Bernstein
PHOTOGRAPHED BY: Oupa Nkosi

In 1994, the year of the mass slaughter of the Tutsi in Rwanda by ethnic Hutu extremists, Alphonse Nahimana was a 24-year-old living in Kigali with the Tutsi mother of his two-year-old child. He was the youngest of six children, identifying as 'mixed race', since his mother was Tutsi and his father, a Hutu farmer. All his family members had died in the genocide or in the refugee camps in Burundi or the Congo, save one brother who, he would later discover, was alive and in jail in Rwanda. After the genocide, Nahimana traversed the continent, trying to create a life for himself. He finally arrived in South Africa in 2001. He worked as a car guard in shopping centres in Johannesburg for many years, but recently found work in a small library in the city.

I do not understand why God lets bad things happen to human beings. If we say we are all in God's image and then you see that God's image destroyed by some other God's image and then God keeps quiet and lets it happen, it's confusing to me. And then we read the Bible and we hear from the preachers and pastors that we are all equal, but then I go to sleep under the Mandela Bridge and someone else goes to sleep in Sandton? Then you tell me we are equal? I don't understand.

We are equal where? We are equal in which situation? Even in education we are not equal. Our lifestyle is not equal. It confuses us and that's how we fight, that's how we become jealous, that's how we kill each other, how we hurt each other. Because we are not equal. We discriminate against each other. That's how racism started. That's how xenophobia started. When you finish eating you throw the bread in the dustbin and somebody else comes to look for that bread in the dustbin. Do you think you are equal to this person?

Inequality is an example of what affects my faith. It's a question I have. Where is God when something bad is happening?

JUMPING OVER BODIES

By 1994 I was living in Kigali and helping my brother in his business, where we exported and imported goods, the kind of goods you might find in a supermarket. I used to travel in Rwanda, Kenya, Tanzania and the DRC. I wasn't involved with politics. Life was good. We were living in a peaceful country and everybody was happy. I was a Christian and enjoyed going to the church. The genocide changed everything.

I realised there was going to be trouble when we heard on the radio that the airplane that President Habyarimana was travelling in was shot down. After that, some of those people, those killers – they were looting. They were destroying the shops and houses.

I was in Kibuyu doing business when the shop was looted. When I came back to Kigali, I found nothing; everything was upside down. After looting our shop, they also went to my house, which was about ten kilometres away, and destroyed it. My wife wasn't in the house, but I knew everybody had run to the church so I went to look for her there. We stayed together for a few days in the church and from there we fled. Although in my ID document it was written 'Hutu', after my father, I was in danger because I was trying to protect my wife, who was Tutsi.

In the four years leading up to the genocide, the Rwandan Civil War had pitted the Rwandan Armed Forces (FAR), led by the Hutu-dominated government of President Juvénal Habyarimana, against the Rwandan Patriotic Front (FPR), a Tutsi rebel group. While peace accords had been signed in 1993, the assassination of Habyarimana on 6 April 1994 sparked the genocide which would leave an estimated 800 000 people, mostly from the ethnic Tutsi minority, dead in just over three months.

It was in July 1994. We left Kigali early one morning, around 3 am, with my wife and daughter. The FAR soldiers were announcing everywhere that people must move away from the city because it was taken by the FPR so everybody must go.

Imagine thousands of people in the road carrying stuff on their heads, carrying bags with the only aim to be away from the country. I was carrying a bag with my clothes and other stuff, and my wife was carrying a mattress on her head; she had our child on her back in an *ingobyi*. If we slept, it was on the road. The sound of bombs and gunshots were all around us. Children were crying, soldiers were chasing and shooting at us, people were dying; all the way to the border people were dying like flies. We had to jump over dead bodies. We travelled like this for a week, walking day and night. The FPR was using live ammunition and chasing us. If you heard the sound of a gun you would just run, leaving everything.

Then what I remember is the sound of a grenade. That's when the shrapnel hit me in my eye. I ran, my eye bleeding. I don't know what happened to my wife and child. You save your life if you can. There was no care; there was no hospital. You just run and go. I must have lost consciousness.

WAITING FOR GOD

I was taken to hospital by the FAR soldiers, who had taken all the injured people, and two months later I found myself in the hospital in the refugee camp, Nyangezi, in the DRC. I couldn't remember anything. That's when I started realising that my wife and daughter must have died. The last thing I remember was her asking me where we were going.

In the refugee camp there were many thousands of people and there was no sanitation. It was dirty, smelling and there was cholera. I stayed there for almost two years. Sometimes, I would go to the nearest village to look for a job, to exchange work for food. But it's not like you are waking up with a plan. You do whatever comes in your mind. In my old life I had a daily plan, an agenda. In the camp there is no agenda. This felt like prison for me. There is no freedom. There is no way forward in the camp; just sitting and waiting for the sun to set and so I can go back to sleep.

But then the FPR started to attack the camp. We were forced to run away, to run into the forest. It was full of people but there was no help, there was no more UN. I stayed in the forest for six months. There was no food but there was too much rivers, too much water. Whatever you meet that is edible, you eat. It could be grasses; you kill animals, there's too much monkeys, there's snakes. You are living worse than an animal because even the animals were running away from us, hiding themselves. You don't know even if it's night or day. No one was wishing to live. I finally reached a point where I cannot find water or anything to eat so I decide to lie down and sleep in the forest and wait for God to decide what's going to happen to me.

After three days, some Congolese, sent by the UNHCR, found me. I thought they were coming to kill me. I stood up and tried to run away. One of them said in Swahili, 'No, don't run, we are coming to rescue you.' That's how I got out of the forest to Kisangani. I think God helped me to get out from that forest.

From Kisangani, the other refugees were taken back to Rwanda by the UN. I pretended to be Congolese – I spoke Swahili – so as not to be taken back. I joined a Congolese group waiting to be taken to the south of Congo, and I went with them to Bukavu where I stayed for four months with a family.

From the DRC, Nahimana headed for Tanzania, where he lived in another refugee camp for several months. In 1998, he travelled to Kenya, making a living in Nairobi, selling shoes. But he kept moving: Malawi, Mozambique and then Zimbabwe. In 2001, when Zimbabwe's political and economic crisis worsened, he jumped the border into South Africa.

IF THEY FIND OUT I AM A FOREIGNER, I MIGHT BE NEXT

When I first arrived, I went to Home Affairs in Johannesburg to apply for asylum. I slept almost a week outside but I couldn't get in because I did not have money to bribe. Then I heard some people there speaking Swahili and they recommended I go to Pretoria. I didn't have money so I walked there; it took me two days. After many days of sleeping outside in the queue I got the papers.

Luckily I met another homeboy who was working as a car guard in Kempton Park and the guy introduced me to the supervisor and I started life working as a car guard in Kempton Park.

At the time, I was staying in town with some Tanzanians, seven of us on the roof of a building near Bree Street. I would travel on the train from town to go to work in Kempton Park. One day I saw some men throw this guy off the train. He did nothing to provoke this. I heard them use the name of *kwerekwere*. I was thinking if they find out that I am a foreigner, I might be next. I was scared of losing my life. That's why I pretended to be deaf. I knew if I spoke, you will know I am not South African. I don't know formal sign language, but if I was approached by someone, I would shrug my shoulders, shake my head, looking confused, putting my hands up until the person knows that this person can't speak.

Even until now, every time I use public transport I know exactly where I'm going, and the price. I bring the right change. I don't want to ask for change. I don't want to talk to anyone when I'm in a taxi.

I remember one day a foreigner was robbed in the taxi. This guy was sitting in front of me. I was in the back seat. He answered the phone and was speaking Portuguese. The people next to him saw his phone was a nice one and they robbed him right there in the taxi. One of the guys had a gun and they robbed him at gunpoint. No one helped him, and the three guys took the phone and his wallet and jumped out at the robot. The scariest part for me was that everyone was keeping quiet and no one would intervene. All somebody said was, 'Ah, *kwerekwere*.'

It's the same story with the police. Once the police stop you, normally they greet you and ask for a licence or ask a few questions in their language. When you respond they will know that you are not South African.

Then they ask you where you come from. Obviously you say where you come from and you try to use the paper. You are now cooked food to eat because no matter how big the document you have, you still must buy cold drink, which means you must pay them. Or they say to you we must talk nicely. To talk nicely is another language of police officers when they want something; it's their way of bribing us without stating it. We are not happy about that, but we don't have a choice.

In 2009, I was waiting at the robot for it to turn green. The police came to me and said, 'Where do you come from?' When I told them Rwanda, they asked for a cold drink. I said, 'I don't have money to buy you cold drink. Even me, I'm looking for cold drink.' Then they arrested me. When they reached the police station they wrote that I was loitering. I didn't even know what it meant but I slept in the cell and in the morning they opened the cell for people to go to court and one man said to me, 'Go.'

The police assume every document for the foreigner is a fake. You must have money to bribe police officers and Home Affairs officers, meaning if you walk with empty pockets you are at risk. This is for every foreigner, not just me.

Corruption is killing the country but at the same time it's helping people survive. I can be honest there. They are making their own living through corruption. They get extra money. They build their own houses. That's how corruption has become like a business. Everyone who has a chance to get a position, especially in the government, they take as much as they can while they are there. Once you get a position, you definitely want to take advantage of that.

YOU CAN BE POOR. BUT YOU ARE POOR IN YOUR OWN COUNTRY

My life changed in 1994. There were no brothers and sisters anymore. People used to kill their own wives; they used to kill their own brothers because they are not the same tribe. So, for me, I didn't even feel like calling myself a Rwandan because I was shamed by people who are human beings and who killed other human beings. Even now sometimes I don't feel like being Rwandan because I'm ashamed.

Some of my family died in the genocide and others died in exile. Some in Burundi, some in Congo, where they were looking for a future. I've got one brother who's in jail now in Rwanda, and I have one cousin and one nephew. The rest of the family is dead.

What makes me sometimes angry is that, it's like if you don't speak any South African language it means you are a foreigner but automatically they will say you are from Nigeria. Some of the South Africans believe we are all Nigerian and Nigerian today means something else – it means corruption, drugs, all those kind of rubbish happenings here with the Nigerians. They don't know how to differentiate between refugees or other foreigners who are here for other reasons. To some of the South Africans, especially when you go to townships and villages, always you are *kwerekwere*.

HOTEL RWANDA

In 2004 they were making the film *Hotel Rwanda* in Johannesburg. I heard from one of my homeboys that they were looking for people from Rwanda, Burundi, Congo, Uganda – people who can speak Kinyarwanda, Swahili and French – to be extras in the movie.

In the film, I played the Hutu's role and was dressed in the uniform of the *Interahamwe*, the militia who was killing Tutsis in the genocide. We had to hold guns and machetes. I didn't like to do it because it reminded me of what's happening in 1994. But because of life and money we have to do it. It's like we didn't have a choice.

Some Rwandans, they refused to work there. They don't want to wear the uniform acting like killing people. Just imagine wearing this uniform, the same uniform those people were wearing and you are now wearing that uniform of the people who were killing.

I became traumatised. When I'm sleeping, I see myself in this uniform; I would have bad memories, flashbacks, bad dreams. I felt sad and confused sometimes, because I don't know exactly what I'm doing there but somehow I came to understand it's not real, it's a movie and we are looking for a living and we also need to show the world that it's happening.

In 2012, so many years after making this film, a Rwandan homeboy told me about my picture on the Internet, on the website of the Rwanda National Congress (RNC), the opposition party founded by exiles in 2010. I went online and found the picture of me from the filming of *Hotel Rwanda*. This article had me on the Internet as a killer. Someone took that picture of me from the film and posted it on the Internet saying that this man was *Interahamwe* and accused me of being a spy against the RNC. Those who are not a member of this party are seen as the enemy, as spies.

They wanted to further their political agenda and destroy my image because I didn't want to join them in their party. After this picture was on the Internet, I start receiving intimidating phone calls saying, 'We know you, we know where you stay and we know all your movements.'

One day, in 2013, I went out to buy airtime in the *spaza* shop down the street. A white City Golf stopped on the street near to my door and three guys came out of the car. One of the guys showed me a police badge and one of them showed me a gun. Then they came behind me and grabbed me and forced me inside the car and drove down the highway straight into City Deep. At the robot, a woman who was waiting for a lift approached the car window, so when I see they are busy talking to that woman, I opened the door, jumped out and ran to safety.

After the kidnapping, I changed my life, my place, my movements. I became isolated and much more careful about where I'm going. I try to be more careful, meaning I must know who I talk to. I must know where I chill out and with who. If I'm outside, for example with the people in a gathering, I must make sure how I'll be going home. I can't say when I'm going because I don't know who's going to attack me on my way. If yesterday I go home this way, today I must go home another way.

My documents were stolen when I was kidnapped and when I went to renew I was told that my file was missing so I could not renew. I didn't want to go and start zero because I was afraid of being rejected, because now Rwandan refugees are not getting any documents because there is a law that could come into being which could mean that all the Rwandan refugees must go home because everything is fine, the country is peaceful. With the Refugee Amendment Bill, as a refugee you have to prove why you are not going back, especially those ones who left in 1994.

The documents I live with now is an affidavit and letter from the Lawyers for Human Rights, which are temporary papers. This means I can't do anything that requires ID. I can't open an account or travel by airplane. I have to live within those limits and try to live a life that doesn't require documents. I always have to be aware of the police, and I have to be careful to not commit crime because then they could deport me.

I didn't want to go forward like I did. I wanted to go back home. My country was a beautiful country, it was peaceful. I enjoyed living there. But I found myself in the situation where I'm not able to go back – I can't go back because I don't see myself in the new Rwanda. It's a dictatorship. People are running away from that dictatorship. It's not peaceful the way they say. I think Home Affairs has to understand the situation in the country now. The Rwandan politics back home are not good for people who are outside the country. If you don't want to go back home the Rwandan government think you are hiding, wherever you are, that you might be part of the genocide. If I go back I can be arrested. I can be killed.

Let me say, I have a friend who had a car accident while she was sitting as a passenger in a car. Now she chooses to never travel in the car as a passenger. It is a trauma. Me, I'm always going forward without a destination.

GENOCIDE STORIES

In 2014 the children at the Hillbrow Theatre were performing a play about the genocide. It was about a man who was Hutu who was married to a Tutsi woman. His family did not appreciate that, and they rejected that woman. I was invited by Gerard Bester, the director of the project, to help by telling the children stories about the genocide, about Rwanda and about the Hutus and Tutsis. I told them about my life and how I came here and the reason why I came and how I survived. When I was telling them my story, they wanted to cry.

They didn't know about Rwanda. They didn't know about Africa in general. When I told them that I walked from Johannesburg to Pretoria they didn't believe it.

It was painful to them, but also it makes them understand. Then they were feeling sorry for some of the foreigners who are refugees. Now, if they meet somebody they will know, 'Oh, we heard the story about Rwanda, about Burundi, about Africa, now we understand.'

I think it is the lack of education. If it's possible for South Africa to know about foreigners and about other countries, and the history of those countries, then they will know if I say I'm from Rwanda, they will know exactly why I'm here. They'll know I'm a refugee, not just a foreigner.

No one would wish to be in a foreign country when your country is peaceful and stable and you can do whatever you do in your country. You can be poor, but you are poor in your country, in your homeland, in your house.

THREE WISHES

When I was about ten years old, around 1977, I remember one of the stories I heard sitting around the fire with my family. It was called 'Three Wishes'.

There was a husband and a wife; they were poor, poor, poor. One day they were sitting at the fire and then God comes and they asked God to give them three wishes so God does.

The woman says, 'This fire is nice. I wish I can have meat to cook.' Her wish is granted. The husband says, 'No you are stupid. We are poor. You should have wished something better. I wish that meat can cover your mouth then you won't speak again. You are stupid. You are a woman.' The meat covered her mouth.

This left them with only one wish. So, because the husband loved the wife, he did not want the meat to stay and cover her mouth forever and he said, 'I wish the meat can be removed from your mouth.' The poor people remained poor and the wishes were finished. They didn't even eat the meat. They wasted their wishes and nothing changed for them.

In 1996, when I was in the bush in Congo, that was the time when I started to understand this story. I wanted to put wishes to God that

God would help me in that situation. I understand how those poor people were feeling.

We ask ourselves, if it was me which wishes would I make? If I could have three wishes now I know only that my one wish would be to have peace of mind, then I can be a peacemaker.

12

I WON'T ABANDON JEPPE

Charalabos (Harry) Koulaxizis

AGE WHEN INTERVIEWED: 43
BORN: Harare, Zimbabwe (then Salisbury, Rhodesia)
INTERVIEWED IN: Jeppestown, Johannesburg, South Africa
INTERVIEWED BY: Tanya Zack
PHOTOGRAPHED BY: Mark Lewis

The son of Greek immigrants, Charalabos (Harry) Koulaxizis grew up around the family engineering business in Jeppestown, where he would go every day after school. In 1996, he and his father opened a catering equipment company with its warehouse headquarters in the same area, just across the road from the Wolhuter Hostel, a barrack-style, single-sex housing facility designed by the Johannesburg City Council in 1932 to house 3 500 migrant labourers, mostly Zulu men. Currently more than 6 000 men are estimated to live in the neglected and decrepit building, which has become a node of violence and illegal activities. In April 2015, Harry's catering warehouse was 'hit' during the spate of xenophobic attacks which had flared up throughout the country.

It was 14 April 2015. They were sitting in groups near the hostel, on all the roads, everywhere. They were toyi-toying in front of the hostel, burning tyres, stoning cars. They were holding pangas, knives, sticks, knobkerries, hammers. A lot of people, jumping up and down, dancing, shouting, screaming. Shirts were off. It was a whole commotion.

I had guards in the place before that – two security in the day and two security at night. But I went to the station commander that day and he said, 'I advise you take these guys out. They can't sleep here. If they sleep, they're gonna kill them.' I felt to myself: You know what? Just imagine these guards die for a few thousand or million rands' worth of articles? I can always replace something but I cannot replace a human life. How would I explain to their families if they had died in my building, protecting my assets for some stupid little toyi-toying? So I decided to withdraw the guys.

Later on, when I went to go close the building, the people from the hostel – they stoned my car. I drove to my building, locked up and put the alarm on. In the middle of the night I came back and was checking what's going on and saw they were burning tyres. The next night they broke into other shops. Took some cars out and burnt them. They even burnt the one shop – went inside and put down petrol bombs and burnt it down.

LET'S LOCK THE BASTARDS IN

My attack happened the following night. It was early morning of the sixteenth. At 2:15 am the alarm got activated. I was asleep at home and I got a call from the alarm people. 'It's a break-in. They broke the front door. They broke the gate; they hooked it with bakkies and taxis and they pulled it open.' I got dressed, got in my car and went to the scene.

While I was driving to the building I was calling the cops. The Flying Squad.

They said, 'The cops are already there, don't worry, everything is in order.'

I said, 'But it's like they already in my building.'

They said, 'Ah, they lying to you, what-what.'

It took me about eight minutes to get to Jeppe and when I arrived there I could see people coming in and out, looting my building. I'm not a vigilante, I'm not a superman. It was a big crowd, and when I say 'a big crowd', you cannot believe. They were running out with our stuff.

I said to the cops, 'Hey let's go get them!'

They said, 'It's too dangerous. Not enough members to go there.'

I drive up to the building myself and throw a stun grenade. Because I'm also in the security business I've got some things like this in my vehicle. But they were still running out of the building. With my articles! So I reversed back because they started firing shots at me. They were shooting at me!

I went to the police who were in patrol vehicles there and tell them what is happening.

They say, 'Ah, there's nothing you can do; let them take what they must take. No, we not going to risk our lives to do what you wanna do.'

I said, 'Call the army!'

They said, 'No, no, no, we are leaving.'

They left me alone from like 2:30 am. So basically, I allow them to take what is here to take. I must risk my life, I must die for three and a half, four and a half or five and a half million? I had my bright light on my car and watched my stuff going.

Eventually, a couple of police from the special unit arrived and the policeman said, 'You have chains?' I've always got chains in my car, not for my building but for my clients' buildings for my security company.

He said: 'Let's lock the bastards in. Then, in the morning, we get more clout and more policemen and we enter the property.'

I jumped into their vehicle with the chains and locks. They put in rubber bullets and start firing them down the road towards the hostel. Hey, we battled there. They pushed them back for me to go to the building and lock it for the time being. I put a new chain there. I was wearing my bulletproof vest.

At 6:15 in the morning the police came from all over. There were about 150 policemen by then. They pushed the people into the hostel; blockaded that road. Round about lunchtime, with members of the SAPS, about 20 of them, we entered the building.

We thought they would be inside, but there was nobody there. They broke the window at the back and escaped; they had emptied the stuff from the back. Some of my stuff was still lying outside – they got scared and dropped some of those articles outside. It was like a World War II inside there. Big chaos. Whatever was left was broken. I nearly collapsed.

THEY TRIED TO MAKE SURE WE WON'T COME BACK

I end up sick for three or four days; I couldn't understand what the hell is happening. You can feel a lotta things at a time, you know what I mean? Hate, you know? Why me?

When my father came to the warehouse a few days later he nearly collapsed. We had to carry him, put him in the car, take him to the doctor. Because he was like, finished, you know? From that day he has never been back to the warehouse. He was too upset. It took ten years of his life, what happened in the space. I don't want to lie. It's different when you're selling it yourself having said, 'I'm gonna retire or I'm disposing my assets.' Making your own choice. Not forced, stolen by locals, South Africans. There was no foreigners that stole.

I can vouch and I can say it was Zulus only. I will explain to you. When they looted inside there, when they were bending down, they must have dropped some of their cellphones. So I picked up the cellphones two days later. Because the three cellphones that we found: all tenants from the hostel. I traced the phones. The other one was staying by the taxi rank.

We got cameras. We had footage. We froze the camera footage and we counted about 700 people. They were vandalising. Just vandalising! The others were stealing. Whatever they couldn't take they broke. They took a DV board off the wall and broke it. And phone lines. That cost us like R28 000. You understand? They cut the power and electricity. To make our lives difficult, you know? They tried to make sure that we don't come back.

I had 11 cars at the time. Destroyed all of them. They stole the beading, they broke the benches, took the bumpers, stripped the car, pulled the cables, pulled the dashboard, took the radio. They were breaking and damaging and stealing. They took ice cream machines, microwaves, dishwashers, vegetable cutters, chicken grillers, fan motors. My father's tools from his lifetime of working. We are talking about over 1.5 million worth of tools. All stolen. All in all, it was about 4.5 million damage.

This is not a xenophobia, it was typical criminal activity.

THERE'S A DREAM

Koulaxizis's father immigrated from Greece in 1967 and his mother followed in 1971. The apartheid government embraced skilled white foreigners – his father was trained as an engineer, his mother a bookkeeper – offering assistance and residency to those willing to come to the country.

In my childhood we stayed in Yeoville. We stayed in a block of flats – four flats or six flats. One side was my mom and dad, the other side was my godmother. Upstairs was my godmother's aunty. So basically it was like a whole family flat, you know?

I grew up on the corner of Rockey and Raymond in Yeoville, where all the drug dealers currently sit. That time Yeoville was still a paradise. Not like now. Oof, you cannot believe it. There's a dream. It was clean streets, people used to walk freely at night, you could go to the Yeoville pool and swim. We played until midnight, 11 o'clock at night, at that time. Could walk around at two in the morning.

It was different people: Greek, Portuguese, Italian, Spanish, Germans and Jewish. A lot of Jewish. I had a Jewish girlfriend for about ten, 11 years. We broke up because I didn't want to become Jewish.

I spoke Greek at home and my father's friends all spoke Greek. That's why I still have an accent. So I feel Greek and I feel South African. But you know what? I would rather do business with a South African than do business with a Greek.

In 1990 I opened my first business in Yeoville. Me and my cousin and another English South African guy, we opened a bar, we had shares, we had a small arcade, we were making money – you know, this and that? Until the end of 1991 I still had that business. I ended up having seven shops in Yeoville. I also had a shop in Illovo. But I didn't enjoy the crowd. It was very white at the time, very posh at the time. It was not for me. I moved out. I worked for an estate agency and for about a year I had a nightclub in Northcliff. I sold it all. I think it's the hours. It was killing me. I had a lot of shops and bottle stores in all kinds of different places. I was buying and selling properties – plus I had the catering business in Jeppe and the security company.

Whatever happens, we are all part of one business, one family business – my sister, myself, my mom, my father. We had it as a warehouse for catering equipment at the time of xenophobia. We had 20 years of assets. The whole place was full of equipment. So it was storage, basically.

You cannot open a retail business here in this area because the minute you open they will stop you and ask, 'How much this?'

'R5 000.'

'How much this?'

'R10 000.'

'How much this?'

So they check who goes inside there with R5 000 for equipment, and bang! – there is R5 000. Bang! if a black person walks in and they see him carry equipment out to his bakkie.

'You know, I asked, and this thing was R5 000.'

Boom! You get shot and killed for R5 000. They do not have value for life, they could kill for R5.

HIJACKED

There is nothing that really brings a real income into this area. The only income is stolen stuff because there are scrapyards, pawnshops. They steal during the day and night and they go and sell at the pawnshop. The police don't do nothing about it because they are scared themselves. There's no streetlights here because they steal the cables. And there are all of the illegal activities. Like firearms, guns. It is well known that Jeppe sells firearms. Sometimes cars get hijacked and they find them here. The last robbery was not so long ago. The cops killed the three robbers inside a building here. So it is a lot of criminal activities.

The hostel was built only for workers. If you passed here during the day in the eighties, nineties, you would not find anybody in Jeppe hostel because if you didn't work, you couldn't stay here.

People that stay around the hostel are trying to educate themselves – to become a nurse, a secretary, to study something. You know we used to help them sometimes when I used to have my office there.

They say, 'Can you print this CV for us? Can you help us with a copy?' We used to help them, give it to them, no charge.

I used to say, 'You know what, one day when you get work you buy me a cold drink.'

End of the day, there's no one to assist them, even for a CV. They don't have money to print a CV. Build a centre. Please. I mean the government is eating so much money. Left and right. Planes, holidays, hotels, entertaining themselves and everything else. They say there's unemployment. But help the people to go get a job. I mean, there's a lot of buildings that are vacant. Convert them to accommodation. Put them in good order.

I have told the guys to clean up the building opposite there because it is looking so bad.

I said, 'You know what? I can give you 20 litres of paint. You can paint the building. I mean you guys are sitting there the whole day. Paint just makes the area look better.'

'Sharp, no problem, we will do it.' They took the paint and they sold it. So, what do you do?

Since the late 1980s, many buildings in the inner city have dramatically deteriorated as banks continue to redline the area, longtime landlords flee and opportunistic slumlords exploit poor tenants unable to afford high rentals, permitting overcrowding. In some cases these buildings are illegally invaded and controlled by strongmen in what is popularly known as building hijacking.

They will take anything vacant, like this building across the road. There was a Nigerian guy there, renting. He had a panel-beating business. He was paying R10 000 a month – on time and everything. He was a nice tenant, you know what I mean? But there were problems every day. 'Hey you bloody Nigerian, hey.' People used to come and intimidate him.

Three days before the attacks they broke into his shop again. One week before that, they took all his tools. So they forcing him to get tired and leave the area – they going to hijack the building. The time of xenophobia, they gave him one hour to move all his cars out, or they going to burn them. Less than 45 minutes, he took like 30 cars with trucks pulling them. Towed his vehicles up and left them on Jules Street. They burnt 25 cars. He's gone. Moved out two days later.

In the hijacked buildings rent comes, whatever rent they are paying – R300, R400, R200 per room – for a squatted room. There is nobody – let me tell you something – there is nobody staying for free. Even if it is R200, you gotta be paying somebody. So now the hijacker provides electricity, he is paying someone from City Power to come and make an illegal power connection. So you gotta pay the hijacker. I mean, he is the boss here. He needs to buy food for himself. He needs to buy something for the honey, correct?

Around the squatted buildings urinating is the biggest problem because there are not enough water and no facilities in most of the

hijacked buildings. So they shit, sorry my French, they shit at night in buckets and in the morning throw it in the streets, in the drain. And they do not pay for services so they can't get a dustbin.

I got a building up the road here I can show you. There's a hijacker there, and he is a very racist guy. They trying to open a case against him.

He says, 'All you fucken white people must get off my place. You can't tell us what to do: this is a black country.'

The police was there last week. There's nothing I can do, because the police is Zulu and he is a Zulu. But he called me a fucken white person, I must fuck off of this country. I was born here, I've got my blood here. My children are born here, my wife is from here. One hundred per cent. My wife is Indian. They don't speak any other language but English. Where must they go?

You must understand the more properties they can hijack, the stronger they'll become. The more Zulus come from Durban, the more power they have. They hijacked a lot of properties in the area. Now yesterday they hijacked another vehicle because it belongs to a foreigner. They want them to get tired. The more dilapidated the area becomes, the more it cannot be developed.

I employ Zimbabweans, Zulus, Xhosa, Malawians, Pedis, Nigerians and Cameroonians, coloured people, all these cultures in my companies. But the worst culture to work with is Zulus. Their time is their time, their teatime is their teatime. There is nothing wrong with it, but they don't go the extra mile like a foreigner will.

A foreigner will say, 'I need this job. I will wash this car because I need this job.'

Zulus say, '*Hai Baba*. Me? I won't wash your car.'

MEETING THE INDUNA

A few days after the attacks, Harry went to meet with the induna at the hostel in an attempt to reclaim some of the items that had been stolen from his warehouse.

When I spoke to my neighbours and said that I am going to go and talk to the indunas, they said, 'Man, you crazy.'

I said, 'Me, I am going.' I was so mad, but I said to myself I am going to do it.

I went; parked my car. I put my gun in my front. I took two extra magazines and I said I am going to go myself. I didn't ask anyone. I am going to walk in myself. Whatever happens, happens because I was so disgusted when it started happening and I was ready – anything could happen. I don't give a damn. If I was going to die, I will die. If I am going to kill, I will kill. Do you understand?

So I went there. All the black people were like, 'What is this fucken white guy doing here? Is he crazy? Is he a little disturbed? What's going on here?'

I went into the hostel, and I asked, 'I want to see the induna.' He came out. He knows me; I know him. He looked at me and smiled.

He asked, 'What do you want?'

I said, 'I want to speak you about what happened to my property and my assets.'

He says, 'Okay let's go and talk.' We walked a bit; we came and sat outside here and now I am waiting because we had to get a translator to discuss what is going on.

I explain my situation. 'Why you attacking me? I am not a foreigner, okay? My staff here are Zulus. I don't have foreign elements working here.'

In my company there are all ethnicities, but I didn't allow them to work here in this building. Do you understand what I am trying to say? Because I didn't want to cause friction between Zulus and Xhosas, or Zimbabweans or Shangaans, whatever the case. I only kept Zulus here. My others, I never allowed them to come here because I didn't want to cause friction. You don't go shit in somebody else's boat.

I said, 'Ever since I am working here do you ever see a foreign guy working here?'

He says, 'No.'

'So why? I am not employing someone from outside.'

'*Ja*, you have no foreigners working for you here.'

So I say, 'Why are you attacking these places? It is you. Mpandla broke in and I found his phone here – and Ndlovu. What are you going to do to help me to find my stuff? At least give me some of my stuff back, the most expensive stuff because you know where they have gone to. You are the chairman. You are their boss so ask people who took my stuff. I don't care about the damages that they have done.'

The man said, 'I had nothing to do with it. You must speak to them direct and have them arrested yourself.'

Then at the end of the month the police had Operation Fiela – that clean-up operation from different police stations. They hit the hostels to find stolen stuff that were stolen at the time of xenophobia. I went to the police station the next morning and I found a couple of pieces – a microwave, power tools, stuff about the value of R20 000.

Another day, in front of my eyes, I saw someone from the hostel going to sell my stuff at the scrapyard he is walking past. I chased him. I got my stuff back. I found a lot of my stuff there at the scrapyard next door, because they were cutting it up for scrap. But when I told the police to go there, they told me there is nothing that they can do. I couldn't even take my stuff back. I could see my stuff there. I got pictures to prove that that stuff is mine. I couldn't take my stuff.

It was definitely, definitely from the hostel. Definitely criminal activities – they opportunists. Between Jules Street and Malvern in an hour they took something like 57 shops. I've already spoke to the municipality. The councillor was laughing in my face; said to me, 'I don't think you're ever gonna do anything about it, it's just xenophobia.'

I GOT A VISION

Koulaxizis had plans to build residential units above the warehouse, but says police and government inaction and corruption are

hampering his efforts. The catering business has completely closed.
He still owns the empty warehouse, and he has continued with his
security business that operates in Jeppestown and in other parts of
the city. He is looking for other business opportunities, including in
property development in Jeppestown.

I love Jeppe; I love Jeppe, and I think there is a lot of success in Jeppe.
Will be. But, end of the day, with these things always happening, it
will drive people away. It's difficult. It makes you more tired. The
only thing is, the government has to come in, I'm not saying the
hostel must be closed, but must be controlled.

My wife doesn't want me to come here! Last week I bought a
building in Jeppe and basically I didn't tell her anything, it only
came out by mistake. It was last week on Tuesday, so Wednesday
she packed her stuff and went to her family in Durban. She says
she couldn't handle it; only came back this morning basically, you
know? She says, 'I can't deal with you anymore, you know, like –
there are so many other areas! But you go to this *kakest* area to go
buy property!'

But I got a vision; one day it will be better. But she says, 'We got
to get a good insurance because when they kill you one day, at least
my children be looked after.'

I won't abandon Jeppe. I will invest more in Jeppe, but I won't
abandon Jeppe. I still want to grow in Jeppe, to build more buildings
in Jeppe. You know, still I want to help these people, you know what
I mean? It's not like I'm against them or I've got a hate or anything
like this. Because of what they did to me – I mean you can't judge
one person; other people in their lives are good, you know what I'm
saying? So you gotta check it, and carry on with your life. Sweep the
pieces and move on.

13

THE INDUNA

Manyathela Mvelase

AGE WHEN INTERVIEWED: 60
BORN: KwaNomoya, KwaZulu-Natal, South Africa
INTERVIEWED IN: Jeppestown, Johannesburg, South Africa
INTERVIEWED BY: Kwanele Sosibo
PHOTOGRAPHED BY: Oupa Nkosi

Since 1978, Manyathela Mvelase has lived at the Wolhuter Hostel in Jeppestown. Predominately Zulu hostels like this one had been viewed as Inkatha Freedom Party (IFP) strongholds, which explains their politically untenable position in the eyes of the current ANC-controlled government. They are now viewed, particularly by the state machinery, as housing armies of malcontents stoking violence. Mvelase lives in a small, multi-roomed outbuilding adjacent to the hostel blocks and serves as the hostel's induna, a Zulu term which implies a bridge between the monarch and his subjects. To earn a living, he plies his trade as a herbalist and healer.

Leadership is natural, without politics, without white people. Black people understand that there is induna, who lords over them. As induna, I am seen as a sell-out because my stance is always anti-war. But my word only carries weight once the police arrive.

I have been in the leadership committee at the hostel since the nineties, and I have always considered myself a peacemaker and have always discouraged crime. I got here by serving in a committee, resolving conflicts, and that very same committee elected me at a later stage.

The way it works is like this: there are block chairmen for each of the six blocks here. Each block has a committee and the chairmen meet with me regularly. I have a deputy and committee members on each floor. Each floor should have six members but they dodge duty. So, it could be four or three on the floor. In another block, it could be one person. These very dodgers end up coming to us when they have problems to untangle. If you don't fuck up, you stay in leadership until the next person comes along. The others before me were induna until they took their pensions. It's that type of a deal. It's not democratic per se because it doesn't involve open elections with the entire hostel.

It's tough being a leader because all you earn, in fact, are grave insults, the harshest of them coming from gunslingers. I appeal to God to stay protected.

THE RUDE AWAKENING

I was born in 1956 in a place called KwaNomoya, near Weenen, in KwaZulu-Natal. My recollections of Nomoya are that we felt wealthy. My family kept sheep, goats and cows. We had crops. All this livestock, which had ample grazing land, belonged to my grandfather, but some of it was my dad's. My grandfather worked for white people on the farms near Mooi River, but only seasonally, maybe for six months each year. I never went to school at all. My people had strong beliefs around wealth, which for them was centred around livestock so I learnt to herd cattle by first looking after calves.

My father worked the farms like his father, but then he also became a mineworker in Kimberley. I was left in the care of my mother, then my grandmother. My mother, who had a dark complexion like mine, died when I was very young. I was the first-born out of 12 children – he had three children from my mother, three from the second wife, four from the next wife and two from his last wife – and I looked like my father.

We were then moved by the apartheid state to Mashuka, a farm area very similar to Nomoya. It was on the edges of someone's farm, so it was fertile. White people were living off the fat of the land.

I don't remember the year that we moved from Nomoya, but the move from Mashuka to Sahluma was in 1969. That was the year the apartheid government demolished our property. From there, life changed drastically. We had no livestock, no crops. It was a forced removal to a desert where we had to build our house from scratch. By that time, my mother had died, so my father's second wife was looking after me and my siblings and my father had to take up jobs in Johannesburg for construction companies.

Sahluma, where we lived, was a good place but it became overpopulated overnight because of the influx of people who were being moved in from all directions. We were basically like prisoners. The only respite was that we still had time for boyish things like swimming in the river and catching fish. Adulthood, in a sense, was a rude awakening.

HOSTELS WERE PLACES UNDER THE WHITE MAN'S RULE

I came to Johannesburg in 1974. My first job there was working for a building contractor, where I made bricks. It was like a boot camp because we slept in tents. It was like being homeless, or being a refugee in your own country. All these problems the foreigners are experiencing now, we went through them long before.

I first lived with my father, who was also working on a construction site, but later worked for a white man in Bertrams. He was also a builder and I was staying in his yard. But the police found us in the yard and they *pad-trekked* us. I wasn't angry, just destitute. This was life as we knew it back then. And that's how I came to the hostel in 1978.

I rented a bed for about R7 a month. The hostel was very different then. There was less loitering, and the floors were so clean they were shimmery because there was a tight hand keeping things in order. There was the law in the streets, there was the law in the hostel, kept firm by the 'blackjacks'. Back then it seemed oppressive, but compared to the hostels as they are now, it was a decent way of life. If you had beaten somebody up, they'd remove you from your block and relocate you. If you were not cooperative, they'd remove you from the hostel. '*Jy, phuma uit!* You, come out!'

I got here when everybody who lived here worked. If you were lazy, you had a table outside to sell things and your table made you money because everybody else worked.

The older men, which in my case was my relative, used to put our money aside for us. They'd give you what you could spend. When you wanted to buy something, you'd tell your guardian. It's unlike today where young people carry money for themselves as soon as they arrive. Under that system everybody lived a prosperous life, relatively speaking. Everybody bought a cow. Everybody sent money home. It wasn't a choice, it was like a law to keep everybody straight.

Hostels were a kind of place of safety before, at least under the white man's rule. For one, there was no alcohol being consumed on these premises. There was no loud noise. Women were not permitted inside. There are no women in this one, specifically, but I am saying, in general, white people were looking after black people.

Hostels were messed up during the early nineties, that time of violence. One was never ever fully in control after that. In settings such as this, there has to be a figure of authority, who says, 'X, Y and Z should happen,' and it happens. This hasn't been the case since those days, be it inside or outside the hostel.

Mvelase characterises the transition in the nineties from apartheid to democracy as particularly traumatic, full of mass migration, the depletion of employment, violence and disease. It was a transition that, at different times, left him powerless as both a healer and a leader. Although he prefers not to talk about it, a man of his leadership qualities and vast knowledge of the healing arts would have been an important figure in the cultural, predominantly Zulu organisation, the IFP.

THEY NEVER SPEAK ABOUT THE SHELL HOUSE MASSACRE

Jeppe in the nineties was not a site where violence occurred as such, but we would experience it when we attended rallies. If we went to a specific area, people would say that they had been attacked on such and such a day. Generally, the violence was in townships like Soweto and Spruitview, as well as on the train lines.

But the only time I witnessed the violence first-hand was when we were shot at during our march for King Goodwill Zwelithini outside Shell House. There were lots of rallies in that period, relating to the welfare of the Zulu king. We wanted him to have his rightful powers in the new regime and we wanted that cleared up before the elections. In some of these gatherings, the king himself and his prime minister Mangosuthu Buthelezi were there, and other men of authority in the IFP.

On the day of that particular march to Shell House, I made my way back to the hostel as soon as I heard shots ring out. What I remember about that day is that the gunfire was sporadic. It wasn't like there was one long volley of fire. So the tension mounted. I left when there were no casualties as yet. But people had started firing into the air. I was skirting the edges that day because I wasn't well, so you tend to think of self-preservation first. But then the situation escalated and I got the hell out of there.

According to media reports, on 28 March 1994, 55 people were killed around Gauteng, including 19 in downtown Johannesburg and eight outside the Shell House building, in what was a 20 000-strong march. The Nugent Commission was set up to investigate the killings, and it ruled the shootings as unjustified. Eleven people, including some ANC security guards, were later granted amnesty at the Truth and Reconciliation Commission (TRC).

What's sad is that the government never speaks about the Shell House massacre. It was not really resolved. They always speak about Marikana – never Shell House. I can reel off names of people who died from this hostel alone. There was Ndlovu, Nene, Qubu, Myeza and others I can't recall. They said there would be discussions about reparations after the TRC but nothing ever came of it. In my mind, this thing was never resolved because, apparently, Zulu life is worthless.

Even when Jacob Zuma was campaigning here for the ANC in the nineties there were people who asked him how he could do that with a clear conscience when there were people who were maimed, killed and shot. He promised the matter would be resolved.

It was people in the different hostels who reached out to each other in attempts to bury the hatchet. There were meetings after meetings until the violence was squashed. The hostels, at some point, became separated according to cultural groups. AmaXhosa and amaBhaca were considered ANC and amaZulu were IFP, which was inaccurate. We couldn't, as black people, be fighting each other when we hadn't accomplished what we wanted from white people.

HUNGER OR VIOLENCE?

Mvelase explains the violence in the hostel as opportunistic crime. Often residents, many of them unemployed youths, march against the increasing creep of gentrification and the unsanitary state of the hostel, only to end up clashing with the police. Sometimes this spreads to the adjacent properties, most of them businesses owned by foreigners. He says a schism has developed between more politically inclined residents and the figureheads of the past, whose generation he embodies.

I'm in a position of authority to enforce some order, but it is not like people listen to me. These youths have too many questions and they don't accept our advice. But it's not like my relations with the people here are completely sour. I would recuse myself, as I do not get paid for this, if that was the case. I feel like they are a law unto themselves, but they still give you a sense of acknowledgement when you speak to them.

As a leader I am a mediator and a counsel against wrongdoings. When your children are about to break the house rules they don't announce it.

At night, activity is considerably more difficult to control. Police have to resort to rubber bullets, because if you corral the looters on one side of the street or block them, they can evade you by going in a different direction. The looting and burning is not something they do brazenly because they are aware that they are being watched.

I don't agree with the perception that hostel residents are violent and pugnacious. The youths here are opportunistic. If they can get into a store and take food, they will. If they can get into a workshop and find metal to sell as scrap they will. That points to hunger rather than violence. These kids have not killed anyone.

The most traumatic time of my leadership was witnessing the violence that was meted out on foreigners in 2015. I couldn't sleep, thinking of ways to stop this. I felt that powerless. But the only people we can stop are people we can see committing crimes. The person that does something and runs into the hostel is merely making us accomplices to his crime. All we can reiterate is how counterproductive that behaviour is, especially if you are marching for some type of official response.

Business people do come here looking for their property or to complain that their stores have been looted and damaged. There have been cases where some found their goods abandoned outside the hostel. But if we don't know where to look, how do we help them? If a person can identify the offender we can help hand them over to police. We, as leaders, cannot be party to police searches because this place is chaotic and there are too many rooms.

The idea that there are criminals here is also misleading. Criminals are everywhere in this country. If there were jobs, you would be able to separate the criminals from the upstanding citizens. But it's hard to have a moral compass if you are drinking nothing but water for five days. Ten people in the room, only one is working. Don't you think the other nine will turn to crime?

Back in the day, women around here worked in the kitchens as domestics, or in textile factories, but now their only choice is prostitution. Then, it wasn't a case of prostitution on every second street as it is now. Young as they are, when will they reach old age? That's not freedom.

WE'D RATHER RESPECT OTHER RACES THAN LIVE IN HARMONY WITH OUR OWN

As hostel leaders, we do meet some of our foreign neighbours. I always say to them that when white people are prosperous, they always offer charity to their neighbours. Why do we as black people not do the same for each other? Why can't we sit together and exchange skills?

Once, in what was such a positive gesture, a Zimbabwean man named Mlalazi summoned a few of us leaders from this hostel to his house and we had a lovely chat to understand each other's perspectives. Now you can ask me what the end result was? Nothing, as such. We just had a great time at his apartment, you understand? Next time, he knows he will be safe because we know him.

Now some others, you try to have a chat with them, and you can just see that these people have no time for you, because maybe they feel wealthy. What they fail to see is that we are just trying to work out how to be good neighbours, given our different socio-economic circumstances.

There are a few exceptions, but in most cases, no one is willing to walk the extra mile. There is a coloured guy who runs a business here, close by. I said to him in a meeting, 'For you to enjoy a healthy working life here, employ some of these men.' He took that advice. If these people should again decide to protest, you can bet your life he will be safe.

I think that this influx will have a sad ending. When you arrive at a place, you have to get to know the locals and find ways of working hand in hand. The ones from further north, especially Nigerians, they work only with each other. They don't even want a South African security guard, or any little job. It's obviously a slippery slope, because if someone is hungry, you have to find a way of winning them over.

When you try to reach out to a person and they turn their back on you, danger becomes an unpreventable situation. This still happens even today, after the events of last year.

It would be smart of them to call a meeting and so we can make suggestions to each other about how our relationship could improve. But they don't want to. I have never called formal meetings about them either. To do that would be to raise temperatures and influence people negatively. I just stand back and watch. I can only speak about these things in hindsight.

The problem with us as black people is that we do not respect each other. We look down on each other. We'd rather respect other races than live in harmony with our own. People run to wash the feet of white people.

IT MAKES YOU WONDER, DOESN'T IT?

Perpendicular to the hostel's entrance is a building on a bustling street where maskandi echoes from some of the street-side bars. Mvelase points to what looks like an apartment block that is being extended upwards.

The guy building apartments here just spoke to the white person who owns the building and that was that. He started erecting a few floors upwards. Even the people doing the construction are not South African.

I am not saying that he should ask our permission, but it would have made a difference had he come to us and said: 'People, I am building something here, going forward can we be each other's eyes and ears?' Because if they had pulled a few people from inside here into their inner circle, when passers-by wonder what is going on, they would have been able to get a decent response from people in the know. But as it stands people are asking each other, 'What is going on?'

When people were breaking into people's property last year, the white man who owns one shop here said to me, 'Are you being racist? Why is my shop being attacked?'

I said to him: 'But you can see that you are not being targeted because of your race. What we can both agree on is that this is a situation for the police. Why don't we call the police and after that, you and I can discuss how best to solve this problem?'

Around this block, something else that stirred up a lot of emotion here was that somebody opened up a set of rooms here for prostitution, couching it as a bar.

People were quite incredulous that somebody could just brazenly set up shop like that. From what I could gather, it was a Nigerian man that had partnered up with a white man, but the business belonged to the Nigerian guy. This thing was not a scandal to people living in the hostel as much as it was to people living just outside of it. People couldn't believe that someone had the gall to expose children to this, people strutting around naked, soliciting.

When people made enquiries they were told that the place had a licence to operate as a bar, so I guess they have to tolerate it.

It all makes you wonder, doesn't it? About why people in this hostel do what they do.

Timeline

The following is a schematic – an admittedly incomplete account of historic events in South Africa, intended to illustrate Gauteng's underlying socio-political formations as they pertain to some of the issues tackled in this collection.

1855	**Pretoria** is founded by the Voortrekkers as the capital of the new South African Republic. However, settlement long predated their arrival. Chiefdoms such as Mogale's domain (now Mogale City municipality) stretched from north of the Magaliesburg mountains to the south of what would become Gauteng province.
July 1886	**George Harrison finds gold** on a Johannesburg farm. The Langlaagte discovery leads to an influx of speculators, labour and investors into what would later become Gauteng province. The local population is displaced or pressed into labour.
1886	**Johannesburg** is founded. Although the identity of the eponymous Johanna is disputed, Johannesburg's colloquial names – 'eGoli' (Zulu) and 'Gauteng' (Sotho) – clearly illustrate it was 'the place of gold'.
22 August 1894	Mahatma Gandhi founds the **Natal Indian Congress** to fight discrimination against Indians in South Africa. It gradually became a national

organisation, which allied with the African National Congress.

1896 The **migrant labour system** is established, a decade after the discovery of gold in what would become Gauteng. A mix of economic incentive and coercion creates an ethnically diverse labour force from as far away as Lesotho and Mozambique, along with much of the South African highlands.

1900 The **migrant labour system is institutionalised**. The Witwatersrand Labour Organisation is given powers to recruit workers from the provinces of Mozambique, the Transvaal and the Cape. Recruitment of labourers began with the formation of the Native Recruiting Corporation in 1912 and continued until 1977 when it merged with another organisation to become the Employment Bureau of Africa, which continued to operate until the 1990s.

8 January 1912 The **African National Congress (ANC)** is founded, an inclusive party intended to represent the interests of all Africans within South Africa.

1913 The **Natives Land Act No. 27 of 1913** is passed, forcing many rural Africans from farms to work as urban or mine labour.

1913 **Early industrial action** occurs when 9 000 African miners strike at Jagersfontein Diamond Mine after a fellow worker is kicked to death by a white overseer. White employees join in brutally suppressing the strike. Eleven African mineworkers are killed and 37 injured.

24 May 1921   **State oppression of African political mobilisation** unfolds with the killing of the 'Israelites' in Queenstown. The government of General Jan Smuts acts against the Israelites. When squatters fail to comply with police ultimatums, they are arrested and their homes demolished. Soon afterwards the Israelites launch an attack, armed with clubs, assegais and swords. Police respond by killing more than 180 people and wounding 100 others.

May 1922   **White mineworkers strike** over general conditions and the hiring of black workers to replace white employees. Protesters eventually organise themselves into armed commandos, triggering the initial deployment of the newly formed South African Air Force. Official records list the number of dead after the episode as 129 soldiers and policemen, 43 civilians and 39 miners.

1923   The South African government passes the **Native Urban Areas Act No. 21 of 1923,** determining where black people can reside. The increase in the black population in Johannesburg due to forced removals in the countryside and the Great Depression leads to the relocation of black people to Orlando, which became the first township of the South Western Townships (SoWeTo). Other major townships of Soweto are Pimville and Klipspruit.

1926   The **Local Government (Provincial Powers) Act No. 1 of 1926** denies citizenship rights to people of Indian descent.

1927   The **Immigration and Indian Relief (Further) Provision Act No. 37 of 1927** provides resources to assist thousands of Indians to leave South Africa.

1934   The **Slums Act No. 53 of 1934**, ostensibly aimed at improving conditions in poor areas, becomes an excuse for expropriating and evicting people in the name of sanitation.

1936   The **Native Trust and Land Act No. 18 of 1936** (later renamed the Development Trust and Land Act 1936) begins formalising a system of native reserves and authorises the Department of Bantu Administration and Development to eliminate black-owned land surrounded by white-owned land, so-called black spots. The same year, the government passes the **Aliens Registration Act No. 26 of 1936** which places strict control on the immigration of non-whites.

1937	The **Black (Native) Laws Amendment Act No. 46 of 1937** prohibits Africans from acquiring urban land without the governor-general's consent.
1939–1945	The **South African economy booms** on the back of mining and industrialisation. Gauteng is the spatial centre of this development, leading to rapid population growth. Informal housing proliferates around cities, stimulating regional and town planning councils to introduce stringent urbanisation, planning and segregation policies.
1942	The North Eastern Protection League **calls for the abolition of Alexandra township,** one of the few where Africans legally own land. The state offers alternative accommodation and some residents move out of Alexandra. However, many stay. From 1948 on, further settlement of people in the township is controlled, and some freehold property is expropriated. Police raid homes, checking on passes, and residents without the relevant documents are systemically moved out.
1944–1950	**Greek migration** to South Africa in the wake of World War II contributes an additional dimension to the country's white population. While numbering only in the thousands, Greeks become visible as shop owners and tradesmen. Among these refugees from war-torn Europe is George Bizos. Arriving as

a child, he would become a lifelong human rights campaigner and was part of the team who defended Nelson Mandela, Govan Mbeki and Walter Sisulu at the Rivonia Treason Trial.

1945 — Government passes the **Native Urban Areas Consolidation Act No. 25 of 1945,** further restricting African settlement in urban areas.

12 August 1946 — **African mineworkers of the Witwatersrand strike for higher wages.** They continue striking for a week in the face of a brutal police response. Officially 1 248 workers are wounded and nine people killed. Eventually the police and army break the strike.

4 June 1948 — The **National Party wins national elections** and begins instituting radical racial segregation policies. The architects of apartheid would control the national government until 9 May 1994.

1949 — The **Prohibition of Mixed Marriages Act No. 55 of 1949** prohibits marriage between white people and any other racial group.

1950 — To further restrict the growth of black urban populations, the government introduces the **Group Areas Act No. 41 of 1950,** designating urban areas as exclusively white, black, Indian and coloured. This forms the basis for the spatial segregation that will become 'grand apartheid'. This is supported by the **Population**

Registration Act No. 30 of 1950, which racially classifies all South Africans as white, native or coloured. The same year, the apartheid government passes the **Immorality Amendment Act No. 21 of 1950** prohibiting adultery, attempted adultery or related 'immoral' acts (e.g. sexual intercourse) between black and white people.

1952   The **Natives (Abolition of Passes and Co-ordination of Documents) Act No. 67 of 1952** consolidates sub-national pass laws into a single, national system. Under this regime, all black South Africans over the age of 16 are to carry the 'pass book' or *dompas* at all times within designated white areas. Under the law, the Department of Native Affairs forms a regional plan for segregated black townships – black areas that will become Mamelodi, greater Soweto, Tembisa, Sebokeng, KwaThema, Thokoza, Vosloorus, Katlehong, Tsakane and others. The entire area between the Witwatersrand municipalities and Pretoria (except for Alexandra and the new complex allocated to Tembisa) becomes either a white group area or white space.

1953   The **Immigrants Regulation Amendment Act No. 43 of 1953** introduces strict controls, particularly against immigrants from the Indian sub-continent.

26 June 1955	The **Congress of the People officially adopts the Freedom Charter.** Bringing together insights from the ANC and its allies – the South African Communist Party, the South African Indian Congress and the South African Congress of Democrats and the Coloured People's Congress – the charter outlines an ambitious manifesto of non-racialism and social democracy and will serve as a foundation for the post-apartheid Constitution.
1959	The **Promotion of Bantu Self-Government Act No. 46 of 1959** (subsequently renamed the Promotion of Black Self-Government Act and later the Representation between the Republic of South Africa and Self-Governing Territories Act) converts 'tribal lands' into independent bantustans. As all black people are considered citizens of these quasi-countries, they are denied parliamentary representation in South Africa; see also the Bantu Homelands Citizens Act No. 26 of 1970.
1959	**Residents of Sophiatown,** a largely black area in central Johannesburg, **are forcibly removed to Soweto** and occupy an area in Soweto known as Meadowlands.
21 March 1960	A breakaway organisation from the ANC, the Pan Africanist Congress of Azania, stages an anti-pass demonstration outside

Sharpeville police station near Vereeniging, south of Johannesburg. A hostile police force opens fire on the marchers, killing 69 people and injuring close to 200, in what has come to be known as the **Sharpeville Massacre**.

30 March 1960 The **South African government bans the ANC and other opposition parties** under the Unlawful Organisations Act No. 34 of 1960.

October 1963– The **Rivonia Trial** leads to the imprisonment
June 1964 of Nelson Mandela and others among the accused who are convicted of sabotage and sentenced to life. Mandela would remain in prison until the ANC was unbanned in 1990.

1970 Under the **Bantu Homelands Citizens Act No. 26 of 1970**, all black people are considered aliens. No black person qualifies for South African nationality or the right to work or live in South Africa. Urban residence is limited to occupying bequeathed property or by special permission of the Minister of Bantu Administration and Development.

1973 The South African government passes the **Aliens Control Act No. 40 of 1973**. This law exempts the Indian racial group from obtaining permits to travel between certain provinces.

1974 **Soshanguve township is established north of Pretoria** on land originally intended to be part of a bantustan. The name reflects the language groups the government intends will live there: Sothos, Shangaans, Ngunis and Vendas.

1975   **Portuguese immigration to South Africa swells** with the independence of South Africa's lusophone neighbours, Angola and Mozambique. Welcomed with some trepidation by the apartheid government – their Catholicism and Southern European origins make them suspect – they are largely of Madeiran origin. Many have lived in Africa for generations. Once in South Africa they typically leapfrog black Africans to occupy a lower middle-class position as tradesmen, farmers and shopkeepers.

16 June 1976   In what is to become known as the **Soweto uprising**, South African police shoot at thousands of high-school students in Soweto protesting against the teaching of Afrikaans in public schools. Officially 176 people are killed, but many more are likely to have died.

1978   The **Blacks (Urban Areas) Amendment Act No. 97 of 1978** introduces a 99-year leasehold system intended to establish a stable urban labour force. Full ownership will not be attainable until 1986. The law was repealed in 1991.

1982   The **Black Local Authorities Act No. 102 of 1982** establishes local government structures similar to those operating in the South African apartheid 'white areas', granting some degree of local autonomy.

1989	As enforcement of the Group Areas Act begins to wane, **Orange Farm is formed through a land invasion**. Through repeated land invasions, what was once a citrus farm south of Johannesburg becomes one of the largest informal settlements in South Africa.
2 February 1990	State **President FW de Klerk unbans the ANC and other organisations** that have been made illegal under the apartheid regime.
11 February 1990	After 27 years in custody, **Nelson Mandela is released from prison** and officially takes up ANC leadership.
March 1990	**Violence breaks out between supporters of the ANC and the rival Inkatha Freedom Party (IFP)** after thousands of Zulus were moved out of their homes in ANC-loyal areas of south-eastern KwaZulu-Natal. With the white government surreptitiously supporting the IFP, violence between the two parties continues until just before the 1994 general election.
1990s	Throughout the 1990s, **reports of attacks on foreign street traders**, particularly in Johannesburg and Durban, persist.
1991	The embattled Nationalist government passes the **Aliens Control Act No. 96 of 1991**, a highly restrictive piece of legislation designed to protect the white South African minority.

27 April 1994	**South Africa's first all-race elections bring the ANC to power.** The newly elected government launches the Reconstruction and Development Programme (RDP) of 1994 offering, among other services, the promise of housing, in line with the Freedom Charter. The term '**RDP houses**' becomes a colloquialism for free houses provided by the government under a subsidy programme.
27 April 1994	**Gauteng province is created** out of the former Transvaal province. It is geographically the smallest but most densely populated, wealthiest and most politically powerful province in South Africa.
December 1994– January 1995	**Armed youth gangs** in Alexandra township, Johannesburg, **destroy the homes and property of suspected undocumented migrants.** They subsequently march the individuals to the local police station and demand that they are immediately removed from the township.
1995	The informal settlement of **Diepsloot is established** as temporary housing for people removed from farms or environmentally sensitive land. Intended to be small and temporary, it ultimately becomes a sprawling complex of tens of thousands of people.
1996	**The Gauteng population is estimated at just below eight million.** In the same year, the quasi-governmental **Human Sciences Research**

Council (HSRC) estimates the number of undocumented migrants in South Africa at between 2.5 and four million while suggesting it could be as high as 12 million (almost 25 per cent of the country's population at the time). After widespread criticism of their research methodology, the HSRC withdraws its estimate in 2002. Nonetheless, the South African Department of Home Affairs continues to cite these figures until the late 2000s.

October 1996 — The new **South African Constitution grants greater autonomy to municipal and provincial government. The Constitution also promises to 'gradually realise'** many of the promises made in the Freedom Charter, including **rights to employment, housing and services.** These are to be delivered under the Growth, Equity and Reconstruction Plan, an initiative widely criticised as favouring investors and markets over the poor.

June 1997 — After being appointed Minister of Home Affairs in Mandela's unity government, IFP leader **Mangosuthu Buthelezi proclaims, 'South Africa is faced with another threat,** and that is **the SADC ideology of free movement of people, free trade and freedom to choose where you live or work. Free movement of persons spells disaster** for our country.'

November 1997 — In discussing the security challenges of a newly freed South Africa, ANC defence minister **Joe**

Modise announces that 'one million illegal immigrants in our country...commit crimes and are mistaken by some people as South African citizens'.

September 1998   **Two Senegalese and a Mozambican are thrown from a moving train** in Johannesburg by people returning from a rally targeting foreigners as responsible for high levels of unemployment, crime and HIV/AIDS.

November 1998   Overturning highly restrictive apartheid-era legislation, South Africa passes the **Refugees Act No. 130 of 1998** granting refugees and asylum seekers the right to live and work in South African cities. The law is internationally heralded for avoiding refugee camps and promoting self-reliance and integration.

10 December 1998   On International Human Rights Day, **Zackie Achmat and others launch the Treatment Action Campaign** to demand anti-retroviral therapy (ART) for the millions of HIV-positive South Africans unable to access treatment. The organisation later directly confronts then-President Thabo Mbeki, who actively denies the link between HIV and AIDS.

14 June 1999   **President Thabo Mbeki takes over** from President Nelson Mandela as the second democratically elected president of South Africa.

August 2000	**Xenophobic attacks in the Cape Flats** near Cape Town leave seven dead.
September–December 2000	**Xenophobic murders** in Langa, Nyanga, Gugulethu, Milnerton and Bellville South leave 12 dead in Cape Town.
4 October 2000	In the landmark **'Grootboom case'**, the Constitutional Court recognises the challenges of realising constitutional promises to South African citizens, ruling that the state is obliged to take positive action to meet the socio-economic needs of those living in extreme conditions of poverty, homelessness or intolerable housing. Irene Grootboom and other respondents had become homeless after being evicted from their informal housing on private land earmarked for low-cost housing. She died eight years later while still living in a shack.
31 August–8 September 2001	South Africa hosts the **World Conference against Racism** in Durban. The conference concludes with the Durban Declaration which explicitly identifies the need to combat xenophobia and calls on countries to develop national action plans to combat racism, xenophobia and related intolerances.
29 November 2001	An incident is reported in which four white **South African policemen set dogs on three Mozambicans** in an alleged animal training exercise.

January 2002	**Violent clashes between locals and Angolan refugees** leave three Angolans and a South African dead in Milnerton in the Western Cape.
15 April 2002	**Billy Masetlha,** director general of the Department of Home Affairs, **argues that** 'approximately 90 percent of foreign persons who are in RSA with fraudulent documents, i.e., either citizenship or migration documents, **are involved in other crimes as well**…it is quicker to charge these criminals for their false documentation and then deport them than to pursue the long route in respect of the other crimes that are committed'.
2003	The **Gauteng population is estimated to exceed ten million** for the first time.
August 2003	**Father Mario Tessarotto,** from the Catholic Welfare Department in Cape Town, claims to have **buried 28 refugees in 18 months** 'because of jealousy and xenophobia'.
January 2004	In his State of the City speech, Johannesburg mayor **Amos Masondo remarks that migrancy puts a strain on employment levels and housing and other services.**
21 March 2004	On Human Rights Day, the acting high commissioner at the **South African Human Rights Commission** notes: 'Refugees, asylum seekers, migrant workers, undocumented immigrants and other so-called "non-citizens"

are being stigmatised and vilified for seeking a better life. They are made scapegoats for all kinds of social ills, subjected to harassment and abuses by political parties, the media, and society at large.'

December 2004 — Four whistle-blowing guards at the Lindela Repatriation Centre in Krugersdorp report **inhumane treatment and violence against immigrants** at the centre.

18 August 2005 — **Southern African Development Community (SADC) members sign the Protocol on the Facilitation of Movement of Persons.** Originally proposed to create free movement in the region, this protocol allows more limited movements among SADC countries. It has yet to be ratified and implemented.

September 2005 — **Zimbabwean and Somali refugees are attacked** and their property looted in Bothaville, Free State.

August–
September 2006 — **Several incidents target Somalis in the Western Cape.** A group of South African businessmen, taxi owners and landlords loot, torch and break down 14 Somali-owned shops, and vandalise and loot 27 more in Masiphumelele, Cape Town. A Somali shop worker is killed in Delft South and a Somali shop owner is shot and killed, and his assistant wounded, in Dunoon informal settlement. Somali traders claim they are being targeted in an organised

attempt to chase them out of Western Cape townships.

October 2006   **Police in the Western Cape admit that xenophobia, and not criminality, is the main motivating factor** in many attacks on property and people.

12 February 2007   A young South African man is shot by a Somali shopkeeper. In the following 24 hours, **targeted attacks on shops and property lead to the displacement of more than 400 Somali nationals** in Motherwell, in the Eastern Cape.

April 2007   **South African residents chase Zimbabweans from their community** in Zandspruit informal settlement near Johannesburg before torching their homes and businesses. More than 800 are displaced, 112 shacks gutted and 126 dwellings looted. Earlier attacks had occurred in 2001.

May 2007   **Attacks on Bangladeshi, Pakistani, Somali and Ethiopian shop-owners** in Schweizer-Reneke, North West province.

October 2007   Following service delivery protests, **foreign-owned or -run shops are attacked and looted** in Delmas, Mpumalanga, displacing 40 people. Simultaneously, clashes between South Africans and Zimbabweans in Mooiplaas, Gauteng, lead to more than 100 shacks being burnt.

8 January 2008	**Two Somali shop owners are murdered** in the Eastern Cape towns of Jeffrey's Bay and East London.
February 2008	**Somali shop owners are forcibly evicted** from Cape Town's Valhalla Park. Foreign-run shops are destroyed in Zwelethemba, Worcester.
31 March 2008	**Seven people are killed,** including Zimbabweans, Pakistanis and a Somali, after their shops and shacks are set alight in Atteridgeville, near Pretoria.
11 May 2008	Xenophobic violence breaks out in Alexandra, including the **burning of Mozambican national, Ernesto Alfabeto Nhamuave.** Violence spreads to Diepsloot, Atteridgeville, Soshanguve, Tembisa and elsewhere in Gauteng, the Western Cape and KwaZulu-Natal. After two weeks, more than 60 people are dead (including many South Africans) and more than 100 000 displaced. The violence ends only when the military is deployed.
22 May 2008	In Tshwane (Pretoria), **a letter circulates warning foreigners, especially business owners, to evacuate the area by the next day.** An anti-xenophobia march planned for 24 May by the Anti-Privatisation Forum from Soshanguve and Atteridgeville is cancelled due to threatened reprisals.

May 2008	**Camps for displaced people are established across Gauteng and the Western Cape.** At least 30 000 people take shelter in these camps which remain open for months, with people fearing reintegration into the communities that violently expelled them.
20–21 September 2008	The National Executive Committee of **the ANC announces that it will recall President Mbeki** 'before his term of office expires' and the following day, 21 September, Mbeki steps down.
1 November 2008	A splinter group from the ANC form the **Congress of the People.**
14–17 November 2009	**Three thousand Zimbabwean citizens are displaced by xenophobic violence** in the rural community of De Doorns, an informal settlement near Breede Valley Municipality, in the Western Cape. The attackers selectively target Zimbabweans despite the presence of other foreign nationals living and working in the same area.
17 May 2010	Warnings are issued of **threats of xenophobic attacks after the 2010 FIFA World Cup tournament.** Government responds by calling those highlighting the risks as 'naysayers' or 'prophets of doom' who wish to denigrate South Africa's achievements.

2010	**The Gauteng population is estimated to exceed 12 million.**
February 2011	**The Greater Gauteng Business Forum is created** by local traders who feel businesses owned by foreigners are illegal and who threaten 'drastic measures', including violent protests, if its demands for closure of those businesses are not met.
29 June 2011	**Nathi Mthethwa responds to critiques by the African Peer Review Mechanism,** arguing that South Africa does not have a problem with xenophobia.
July 2012	**A South African youth is killed by a foreign shopkeeper.** Katlehong community members respond by attacking the shop owner. Violence spreads across various townships, with widespread looting and displacement.
27 February 2013	Eight South African **police officers** in Daveyton, east of Johannesburg, **tie 27-year-old Mozambican Mido Macia to the back of a police van before dragging him down the road.** The man later dies in a police cell, from head injuries.
26 May 2013	**Further xenophobic violence occurs in Diepsloot.** Two Zimbabwean men are killed.
2014	Statistics South Africa reports that between 1994 and 2014, employment rose by 6.2

million, but the labour force (those working and those seeking work) rose by 8.7 million, resulting in a **net increase of 2.6 million unemployed.** The black African unemployment rate based on the expanded definition had declined from 43 per cent to four per cent, yet there was an additional 3.1 million black African workforce unemployed.

2014   Department of Housing statistics indicate that **South Africa has delivered 2 835 275 RDP houses between 1994/95 and 2013/14.**

19 January 2015   **A Somali shop owner shoots and kills a 14-year-old South African boy,** Siphiwe Mahori, during an alleged robbery in Soweto. Lebogang Ncamla, 23, is also shot three times in the arm. **The incident triggers attacks on foreign-owned shops.**

5 March 2015   **Foreigners** on the outskirts of Polokwane, Limpopo, **evacuate shops after protesting villagers threaten to burn them alive.** Violence erupts in the Ga-Sekgopo area after a foreign shop owner is found with a mobile phone belonging to a local man who was killed.

20 March 2015   In a public speech, **Zulu king Goodwill Zwelithini likens foreigners to lice and demands that they go home.** Violence against foreigners follows soon after.

12 April 2015	Five people are killed as **attacks on foreign nationals continue in** Umlazi and KwaMashu outside Durban, **KwaZulu-Natal.**
14 April 2015	**Looting of foreign shops spreads to Verulam,** north of Durban, **following a day of clashes between locals, foreigners and police in the Durban city centre, KwaZulu-Natal.** About 300 local people loot foreign-owned shops, and only two people are arrested.
April 2015	In response to ongoing violence, the **government launches 'Operation Fiela'** ('fiela' is a Sesotho word that translates in English as 'sweep clean'). Ostensibly aimed at eliminating criminality and 'general lawlessness' it heavily targets foreign residents in poor areas.
April 2015	**The National Joint Operational and Intelligence Structure presents a 27-point programme to address 'xenophobia and immigration issues'.** It includes dedicated courts and prosecutors to deal with xenophobia and immigration and 'improve South Africa's poor record of not punishing violence against foreigners'.
2016	**The Gauteng population is estimated to exceed 14 million.**
4 January 2016	**The South African government presents its National Action Plan to Combat Racism Racial Discrimination, Xenophobia and Related Intolerance for public comment.**

Originally scheduled for distribution in the
wake of the 2001 Durban conference against
racism, the plan notes the challenges of
xenophobic discrimination but offers little
guidance on combatting it.

March 2016   **Anti-foreigner violence breaks out in Mandela,
an informal settlement in Katlehong,** south of
Johannesburg. The shooting and injuring of
three people by a Somali shopkeeper sparks
the incident. In protest against the shooting,
residents in the area loot 50 Somali shops.
The Somali shopkeeper is charged with three
counts of attempted murder and the possession
of an unlicensed firearm.

April 2016   **Foreign-owned shops are attacked and looted
in Katlehong.**

February 2017   **Community members attack homes belonging
to Nigerian nationals** living in Rosettenville,
Johannesburg, ostensibly fighting against drug
traffickers and prostitution.

February 2017   **In Mamelodi, Pretoria, residents mobilise
support for an anti-immigration march** against
the employment of foreign nationals and their
apparent illegal occupation of RDP houses.
They march to downtown Pretoria where they
present demands to city officials.

May 2017   Former president **Thabo Mbeki publicly
denies that anti-foreigner attacks in 2008 and**

since have been xenophobic. Instead, he argues the cause is rooted in poverty and 'township thuggery'.

28 July 2017   Government releases its **White Paper on Immigration,** outlining a range of security and control measures to restrict the movements of refugees and strengthen border controls while promoting the movements of highly skilled labour.

February 2018   **The South African Human Rights Commission holds hearings on xenophobic violence.**

Glossary

African Diaspora Forum An immigrant-run, non-profit organisation established in 2008 to provide a platform for African migrants to voice their concerns and work towards an integrated society.

amaBhaca (sg. Bhaca) An ethnic group of South African people who live mainly in Eastern Cape province. Closely related to the broader Xhosa-speaking population, the group nonetheless retains a distinct identity.

ANC The African National Congress has been South Africa's governing party since the transition to democracy in 1994. Founded in the early part of the twentieth century, the party played a central role in the struggle against apartheid. In recent elections, the party's political hegemony has significantly weakened as it has been charged with corruption, underperformance and nepotism.

Armscor The procurement agency of South Africa's Department of Defence.

atchar A South Asian pickle brought to South Africa in the late nineteenth century, made of seasoned vegetables or fruits preserved in oil, salt and spices.

baas An Afrikaans term used to refer to a boss or master. Historically, it was particularly used by black or coloured people to refer to white people in positions of authority, such as employers.

bakkie A small van with an open body (a pick-up truck).

blackjack A term used to refer to black policemen who patrolled the townships and hostels during the apartheid era, policing pass laws and arresting household owners in arrears with rents.

boer Derived from the Dutch word for 'farmer', the term refers to white Afrikaans-speakers in southern Africa. It is often used in a derogatory sense, referring to those who promoted, sustained and benefited from apartheid.

CBD An abbreviation for central business district, used across South Africa. This typically refers to a city's downtown area but may also refer to a suburban high street.

Chappies A South African brand of chewing gum famous for iconic 'Did you knows' inside the wrappers. Now used generically for all chewing gum.

coloured A racial category developed by the colonial and apartheid governments referring to people of mixed-race ancestry. Although still in use by the post-apartheid government, the term is contested by many of those who have been classified as coloured.

Economic Freedom Fighters A self-proclaimed radical South African political party established in 2013. Originally formed by the former ANC Youth League leader Julius Malema, the party calls for the nationalisation of major strategic economic sectors and the expropriation of land. Although maintaining a relatively small number of seats within Parliament, their theatrics and visibility have made them an important political player.

eish A colloquial exclamation in South African slang used to indicate shock, surprise or resignation.

Eskom A parastatal established in 1923 for the generation, transmission and distribution of electricity across South Africa. Eskom has come under fire for providing irregular service and for irregularities in the construction of new and proposed electricity generation facilities.

Fanagalo/ Fanakolo A South African pidgin with Zulu, English and Afrikaans components. Used as a kind of lingua franca among ethnically diverse mineworkers, it was also the language white supervisors often used to communicate with African workers.

Flying Squad A rapid response unit of the police force.

Freedom Charter Signed in June 1955, the charter is a statement of principles that calls for equality among all those who live in South Africa. Drafted as a response to the injustices of the apartheid government, it inspired the country's 1996 Constitution.

hawker A term used to refer to street vendors, typically those working on foot.

hippo An armoured police vehicle designed to withstand improvised explosive devices and ambush.

Home Affairs South Africa's national department responsible for the verification and protection of the identity and status of citizens and other residents of South Africa including immigrants, refugees and asylum seekers. It has frequently been the subject of legal action by human rights organisations for its treatment of asylum seekers, refugees and undocumented migrants.

hostel Compounds created for black miners throughout the twentieth century as a way to regulate the movement of black migrant workers in urban spaces. The hostels remain part of the country's apartheid legacy and have played a role in the recent waves of violence against foreigners.

induna A southern African tribal councillor or headman who usually addresses the chief or king. The term is also used to refer to the head of a hostel.

ingobyi A Kinyarwanda term for a piece of cloth used to carry a baby on the back.

Inkatha Freedom Party or IFP A South African political party with support coming largely from Zulu speakers in KwaZulu-Natal province. In 1990, political violence between supporters of the IFP and the ANC resulted in the deaths of over 3 000 people. The tension between the two parties continued until 1994 as the former sought to protest the elections. The party's leader,

Mangosuthu Buthelezi, has been accused of trying to derail the country's first democratic elections. Nonetheless, he served as the country's first Minister of Home Affairs during the post-apartheid period. Since this time, support for the party has been slowly declining.

Interahamwe The Hutu militia organisation in Rwanda, which played a central role in the 1994 Rwandan genocide.

kak An Afrikaans term that means 'shit'. It is often used as an exclamation or an adjective.

Khoisan A 'cluster' of two groups of indigenous southern African people, the Khoikhoi and the San. The Khoisan were historically called 'Bushmen' by colonialists, a term that remains contested to date.

knobkerrie A hand-carved, wooden stick with a round knob at one end used for hunting, as a weapon and/or a symbol of authority or status.

kwerekwere (pl. *amakwerekwere*) A usually derogatory term used in many parts of South Africa to refer to foreigners, including immigrants and people of particular ethnicities from South Africa.

lobola A custom commonly practised among black South Africans in which a groom's family must make one or more 'payments' (typically in cash or cattle) to the bride's family. Known elsewhere as bridewealth.

location An informal term used to refer to a township.

magogo (sg. *gogo*) A Zulu word for grandmothers, widely used across South Africa, usually in its singular form.

makula A term used to refer to Asian people and in particular Indians, Pakistanis and Bangladeshi. In the context of xenophobic violence, it is a derogatory term.

malume A Zulu word for uncle. The term is used more broadly to refer respectfully to an older man.

maskandi Traditional Zulu music originating in the early-mid twentieth century during the forced labour migration and as such, the experience of predominantly male migrants' lives in the music.

matric Short for matriculation, this is a term used to refer to the final year of high school and the qualification received upon graduating.

meticais The currency of Mozambique.

MK or uMkhonto we Sizwe Translated into English as 'the spear of the nation', the MK was the ANC's military wing. Launched in 1961 in the fight against the apartheid government, it had bases throughout southern Africa (as far north as Tanzania). MK veterans remain a potent political force.

morogo A collective term designating leafy greens, in particular wild spinach. It is a traditional South African dish and a staple in many communities.

muti A term used to describe traditional medicine in southern Africa. The term is sometimes used in reference to all forms of human and veterinary medicine and, occasionally, to pesticides or other chemicals.

nyaope Also known as *whoonga*, *nyaope* is a highly addictive street drug with varying ingredients including low-grade heroin, anti-retroviral drugs, rat poison, cleaning detergents and acid. The drug is usually mixed with marijuana and smoked or injected.

Oliver Reginald Tambo An anti-apartheid activist and politician who was a founding member of the ANC Youth League and an exiled president of the ANC from 1967 to 1991. He died in 1993, just before the end of apartheid, and is widely revered as one of the country's most important struggle heroes together with Walter Sisulu, Nelson Mandela and a select other few.

Operation Fiela An inter-departmental operation aimed at eliminating crime and general lawlessness. The operation was formed after the 2008 xenophobic violence and became accused of targeting migrants in its raids.

PAC or Pan Africanist Congress of Azania A political party formed on 6 April 1959 due to contestations over political ideologies within the ANC. Led originally by Robert Sobukwe, it drew heavily from pan-Africanist and anti-colonial thought. Although still active, it has struggled to maintain widespread support in the post-apartheid period.

pad-trekked An Afrikaans term that literally means 'farm-walked'. It is widely used to refer to exploitation of people or actions forced upon someone or a group.

panga A variation of machete characterised by a long and broad-bladed knife used as a cutting tool or a weapon.

pap A thick maize porridge, pap is a traditional staple food for many South Africans.

polony A highly processed South African bologna product traditionally dyed bright pink and used popularly in sandwiches.

Reconstruction and Development Programme or RDP A socio-economic policy implemented in 1994 by the post-apartheid government. Informally, the term is used to denote the government-subsidised houses provided as part of the programme's basic services.

Red Ants A private security company used by the government predominantly in evictions of illegally occupied buildings.

robot An informal term used in South Africa to denote traffic lights.

SAPS The South African Police Services.

Shangaan An ethnic group typically associated with southern Mozambique and the eastern provinces of South Africa. In South Africa, members of this group often call themselves Tsonga and actively distance themselves from the broader Shangaan category. In part this is due to the term's derogatory use for people who are seen as poor and uneducated from parts of South Africa's Limpopo province and Mozambique.

sharp A South African colloquial term generally used to express agreement or enthusiasm. Sometimes repeated as 'sharp sharp' to express emphatic agreement.

sister A term used across South Africa to refer to a female nursing sister or charge nurse.

South African National Civic Organisation A national body of civic organisations formed in 1992 shortly before the demise of the apartheid regime. It brought together multiple organisations – often referred to as 'civics' – which occasionally fused political activism with violent protest.

spaza shop A slang term used to denote a small and informal convenience store usually in township areas. *Spaza* shops were often run illegally during the apartheid era when black residents were prohibited from owning businesses in the township. *Spaza* shop ownership is currently the source of tensions between immigrants (typically Somali and South Asian) and black South Africans.

tackies An informal term for sneakers or sports shoes.

taxi A privately managed minibus that carries passengers along set routes. Developed originally to service black residential areas that had limited public transportation options, taxis remain the predominant mode of transport for both long-and-short-distance travel in South Africa.

Telkom A parastatal and South Africa's major telecommunications service provider.

toyi-toying A southern African dance originating from Zimbabwe that became famous for and continues to be used in (political) protests; the term is often used as a synonym for public political protest.

tsotsi A Sesotho slang term for thief, gangster or otherwise dodgy character.

tuckshop A small formal or informal food-selling store.

veld An Afrikaans term for 'field' used to refer to various types of open, uncultivated landscapes.

ZCC or Zion Christian Church Founded in 1910, the ZCC is the largest African-initiated church in southern Africa. Fusing African and Christian traditions, it now has more than four million members.

zol An informal term for a hand-rolled cigarette, especially containing cannabis.

Selected place names

Alexandra A famous and politically charged township in the northeast of Johannesburg. Established in 1912, it remained one of the few sites where, prior to the 1930s, black people could buy and own freehold land. Alex, as it is commonly known, is the birthplace of many of South Africa's artistic and political leaders.

Atteridgeville A township located west of Pretoria with a long history of violence and, more recently, violence against foreign nationals.

Beit Bridge/Beitbridge Twin towns on either side of the South African and Zimbabwean border in Limpopo province. It is the primary crossing point between the two countries and for traffic into and out of much of southern Africa.

Carletonville Carletonville was founded in the late 1930s as part of Gauteng's gold rush. Built around one of the world's deepest gold mines, the area's economy has declined in recent years, along with the region's mineral sales. This has exacerbated social tensions among the area's diverse and dynamic populations.

Daveyton A township east of Johannesburg, established in 1955 by the apartheid government. It is colloquially known as the 'Chevrolet Township' for its collection of Chevrolet models serving as taxis for the local population.

Freedom Park A township located in Soweto, south of Johannesburg. Unlike the older sections of Soweto, it was formed through a 'land invasion' rather than planned by the apartheid government.

Ga-Rankuwa A township situated 37 kilometres north of Pretoria. The area was proclaimed a township by the apartheid government to accommodate those forcibly removed from other parts of Pretoria designated as 'whites only'.

Hillbrow An inner-city, high-rise neighbourhood of Johannesburg that has become widely known as the destination for migrants across South Africa and the rest of the continent. Previously designated as a white area, it was one of the first parts of Johannesburg to see mixed-race residential settlements. Along with its cosmopolitan reputation, it is popularly perceived as a space of widespread criminality and urban blight.

Illovo An affluent suburb located in the north of Johannesburg, the area was founded in the early 1900s and developed a suburban character in the 1930s. It remains primarily white but with a growing population of people belonging to the black middle class.

Jeppestown A light industrial and residential area in the inner city of Johannesburg. The area's single-sex hostels, historically constructed to house black migrant labour, have featured in instances of violence against immigrants and have been raided by the police for stolen goods.

Johannesburg South Africa's most populated, wealthiest and most socially diverse city, Johannesburg is at the heart of the Gauteng City Region (which includes Pretoria and other municipalities across the province). The city was established after the discovery of gold in 1886 and is colloquially referred to by its Zulu name, eGoli, meaning 'the place of gold'. The city itself had an estimated population of 4.4 million in 2016. The Greater Johannesburg Metropolitan Area has an estimated population of eight million.

Kagiso A township located between Soweto and Krugersdorp, to the west of Johannesburg, next to Tshepisong.

Katlehong Located deep in the mining belt, Katlehong is one of the most rapidly growing parts of Gauteng. It was established in 1945 as a small settlement for labourers, but over the years has swelled due to in-migration from across the country and further afield. One of the poorest of the province's townships, it has been deeply politicised and saw considerable violence during the anti-apartheid struggle and continues to see high levels of crime and organised inter-group violence.

Laudium An Indian township located in Pretoria, created by the apartheid government for Indians who had been forcibly removed from other parts of the city. It borders Atteridgeville and there have been regular tensions between the areas' Indian and black residents.

Lindela A deportation centre for undocumented immigrants, located in the west of Johannesburg near Krugersdorp. The centre was opened in 1996 and has regularly been the object of legal action from human rights organisations for alleged ill-treatment of detainees.

Mabopane A largely black township located north of Pretoria, close to Soshanguve.

Mamelodi One of Pretoria's largest black townships, with an estimated population of around 350 000. Located northeast of the city, it is home to one of the country's most famous soccer teams, the Sundowns. In 2017 it was also the site of a mass anti-immigrant protest organised by the Mamelodi Concerned Residents association.

Marabastad A business area located northwest of central Pretoria, with a history of large-scale forced removals in the early twentieth century. It has recently housed one of South Africa's refugee reception offices where would-be asylum seekers make claims for legal status.

Marikana A small town in North West province. The town has become well known for the August 2012 Marikana massacre, when police opened fire on a crowd of protesting mineworkers, killing 34 people.

Meadowlands A township located in the southwest of Johannesburg and established in the mid-nineties by the

apartheid government, during which time black people were
removed from the city centre. It is now one of the oldest areas
of a broader Soweto.

Nomoya A farm area in KwaZulu-Natal acquired in the
mid-1960s for the relocation of black people evicted from
elsewhere.

Northcliff One of the older, more affluent suburbs of
Johannesburg, located northwest of the central business
district. It remains mainly white with large houses overlooking
the city.

Orange Farm Home to approximately 80 000 people, this is one of
the largest and poorest townships, located about 45 kilometres
south of Johannesburg. Founded in the late 1980s by people laid
off from nearby farms, it is one of Gauteng's fastest growing
townships. Among those employed, the vast majority commute
into the city. The township is characterised by frequent protests
and more recently, violence against foreigners.

Orange Grove A racially mixed suburb in the northeast of
Johannesburg. One of the city's oldest suburbs, during the 1960s
it became a primary destination for Italians and Greeks who had
come to South Africa looking for work. It retains strong Italian,
Jewish, Portuguese and Afrikaans representation among its
increasingly black population.

Pretoria Long the heart of Afrikaner power, the city of
approximately three million people is now officially known as
Tshwane. It is South Africa's political capital and houses the
Union Buildings, home of the presidency. It is the third largest
city in South Africa and, together with Johannesburg to the
south, is at the heart of the Gauteng City Region.

Rosettenville One of Johannesburg's southern suburbs, it has long
housed a significant number of the city's Portuguese-speaking
population. A lower middle-class area, its white Portuguese
population helped attract black lusophone migrants from across

the continent. It has more recently become home to substantial Congolese and West African populations. In 2017 it saw overt xenophobic violence in which South African community members burnt the homes and businesses of Nigerians they accused of dealing in drugs and running brothels. It also houses St. Peter's Priory, a historically black boys' missionary school which educated artists such as Hugh Masekela and Es'Kia Mphahlele.

Roslyn A primarily industrial suburb in Pretoria notable as the location of car manufacturers such as Nissan and BMW.

Rustenburg A city of approximately 110 000 people in North West province, it is known for platinum mining. It has long been a destination for migrant labour from across the country and the region. Greater Rustenburg includes Marikana, a town that became infamous for the police killing of 34 mineworkers during a 2012 labour dispute.

Sandton City Located at the heart of Johannesburg's Sandton suburb, this upscale shopping centre is a destination for wealthy shoppers and socialites from across the continent. Situated amidst many of South Africa's corporate headquarters, the centre and its surrounding area are commonly referred to as 'Africa's richest square mile'.

Sophiatown A historically significant Johannesburg suburb that was a major cultural and political hub of the urban black population in the first half of the twentieth century. Famed as a space for inter-racial mixing and its jazz scene, it yielded numerous artists such as Dolly Rathebe and Miriam Makeba. It was also home to some of the country's most notorious gangsters. In the 1950s, the apartheid administration infamously forced out the entire black population into more peripheral suburbs such as Meadowlands. Sophiatown's buildings were razed and the area was renamed Triomf ('triumph' in Afrikaans) and handed over to white residents. Its name reverted to Sophiatown in 2006.

Soshanguve Situated about 25 kilometres north of Pretoria, this township of more than 400 000 was established in 1974. Originally designated to be part of the Bophuthatswana homeland (i.e. bantustan) just to the north, its name - formed from the terms Sotho, Shangaan, Nguni and Venda - reflects the ethnic groups resettled there from Atteridgeville, Mamelodi and other places. It is now fully incorporated into the Tshwane Metropolitan Municipality. The area often makes headlines for drug abuse, crime, protest actions and xenophobic violence.

Soweto An acronym for South Western Townships, Soweto is one of Johannesburg's oldest black areas with parts of the area dating back to the early twentieth century. Soweto grew dramatically as Johannesburg industrialised, and as the townships became a primary destination for black South Africans forbidden to reside in other parts of the city. In June 1976 it saw widespread protest against Afrikaans-medium education, primarily by high-school students. The police fired on thousands of marchers resulting in the deaths of 23 people. It saw continued violence throughout the 1980s and in the 1990s was the site of running, often violent battles between supporters of the ANC and other political parties, most notably the Inkhatha Freedom Party. Today the townships have a largely black and coloured population of over 1.3 million people and is a major tourist destination.

Springs A city located on the East Rand in the Ekurhuleni Metropolitan Municipality of Gauteng, with a long-standing engagement in mining.

Sunnyside A centrally located suburb of Pretoria and one of the city's few areas filled with high- and low-rise apartment buildings. Once hosting a young and affluent white population, it is now a largely black area housing people from across South Africa and the region. Like Hillbrow in Johannesburg, it is a business and social centre for many and a site of fear for others.

Tembisa A township of almost half a million people located in the East Rand region of Gauteng, an area developed primarily to service mining and manufacturing labour needs. It was established in 1957 by the apartheid government as a residential site for black South Africans evicted from other areas. The area is well known for being the province's second largest township (after Soweto) and for its involvement in the June 1976 student uprising.

Tsakane A township of approximately 140 000 people, located in the East Rand area of Gauteng. The area was declared a township in the 1960s during the forced removals of black people from urban centres.

Tshepisong An informal township located in the West Rand region of Gauteng, close to Soweto. It was established in 1998.

Vlakfontein An informal settlement in the south of Johannesburg. Formerly farmland, the settlement is close to the long-standing Indian suburb of Lenasia.

Yeoville Established as Johannesburg's first suburb in the early twentieth century, its position on one of the city's rocky ridges allowed residents to escape the mining town's noise and dust. For many years it was a largely white middle- and upper middle-class area that became known for its cosmopolitanism and leftist politics. Together with Hillbrow, it was one of the first areas of Johannesburg to become racially mixed, creating a nightlife and cultural scene famous throughout the country in the 1980s and 1990s. By the 2000s it had become a primary destination for African immigrants and most of its white population had moved elsewhere. It retains a lively market and nightlife, which is often marred by violence and urban degradation.

Contributors

Ragi Bashonga is a storyteller, poet, sociologist and aspiring academic who has worked in the areas of contemporary black youth identities, gender and creative social movements. She is a PhD candidate in sociology at the University of Cape Town and her academic achievement has been recognised with membership of the Golden Key International Honour Society. She is currently a researcher at the Human Sciences Research Council in Pretoria.

Suzy Bernstein has been involved in various facets of media, including photography, writing and film-making. She has worked in South Africa as a freelance photographer for the last 20 years and has taken part in several exhibitions. Her work has concentrated largely on the arts, although not exclusively.

Ryan Lenora Brown is the Africa correspondent for *The Christian Science Monitor*. Her reporting spans nearly a dozen countries on the continent, with a particular focus on African cities and the lives of the people who inhabit them. She has written extensively about immigration in South Africa and her work is widely published across a range of media. She is a current fellow of the International Women's Media Foundation and the International Reporting Project.

Caroline Wanjiku Kihato is a visiting associate professor in the Graduate School of Architecture, University of Johannesburg, and a global scholar at the Woodrow Wilson International Center for Scholars, Washington, DC. She is the author of *Migrant Women of Johannesburg: Life in an in-between city* (Palgrave Macmillan) and co-editor of *Urban Diversity: Space, culture and inclusive pluralism in cities worldwide* (Johns Hopkins).

Loren B Landau is the South African Research Chair in Human Mobility and the Politics of Difference at the African Centre for Migration & Society at the University of the Witwatersrand in Johannesburg, where he was the founding director. His work, including several publications, explores human mobility, citizenship, development and political authority. In addition to his academic work, he has served as the chair of the Consortium for Refugees and Migrants in South Africa and on the South African Immigration Advisory Board.

Eliot Moleba is a scholar, playwright, theatre-maker and director. His work addresses contemporary socio-political issues affecting young people. He is a member of PlayRiot, a collective of playwrights committed to telling bold, contemporary South African stories. He is currently the resident dramaturg at the South African State Theatre.

Dudu Ndlovu is a post-doctoral fellow with the African Centre for Migration & Society and a Newton Advanced Fellow at the University of Edinburgh (2018–2020). Her inter-disciplinary doctoral dissertation explored Zimbabwean migrants in Johannesburg who are victims of Gukurahundi, the Zimbabwean government-sponsored military operation that resulted in the deaths of approximately 20 000 people in the south western parts of the country. She is also a researcher and writes poetry.

Oupa Nkosi began taking photos in 1998 with a pawnshop camera. After graduating from Johannesburg's Market Photo Workshop, he freelanced, ran community projects, won a Bonani Africa award, and had his work selected for exhibitions in Zimbabwe and Japan. He began his professional career as an intern at the *Mail & Guardian* where he is now the publication's chief photographer. He also writes features for the publication and lectures at the Market Photo Workshop.

Thandiwe Ntshinga is a freelance writer and student of social anthropology. Her research has primarily revolved around whiteness, and she has published about poor whites in South Africa. Currently she is studying at the University of Witwatersrand, continuing her investigation into the ideological significance of poor whites in South Africa.

Tanya Pampalone is the managing editor of the Global Investigative Journalism Network, a non-profit based in Washington, DC, and has been moonlighting as a non-fiction editor for Pan Macmillan South Africa since 2013. The former executive editor of the *Mail & Guardian*, she won South Africa's most prestigious journalism award for creative writing, the Standard Bank Sikuvile, in 2012 and was the 2013 Menell Media Fellow at Duke University's Sanford School of Public Policy.

Nedson Pophiwa is a chief researcher in the Human Sciences Research Council's Democracy, Governance and Service Delivery programme. For the past 14 years he has been involved in numerous academic and policy-focused research projects within South Africa and the region. His main research interests are in good governance, cross-border trade, migration, sustainable development and informal economies, and he has published several peer-reviewed publications.

Greta Schuler is pursuing her PhD in creative writing at the University of the Witwatersrand. Her dissertation focuses on the lives of migrant sex workers in Johannesburg. She is also conducting research with the African Centre for Migration & Society as a doctoral fellow, following her MA in forced migration from the University of the Witwatersrand, Johannesburg.

Kwanele Sosibo is currently an arts writer at the *Mail & Guardian*. He joined the publication as an intern in 2005, after having freelanced extensively as a feature and an arts writer. In 2011, he became the inaugural Eugene Saldanha Fellow in social justice and inequality reporting and has since published numerous long-form features in publications such as *The Con*, *Chimurenga*, *Baobab* and *Rolling Stone*.

Tanya Zack is an urban planner and writer who has operated as an independent consultant since 1991, straddling academic research and practice. Her recent work centres on the inner city Johannesburg. This includes work on migrant spaces and, in particular, on the spatial and economic shifts in Ethiopian entrepreneurial location in the inner city. With photographer Mark Lewis, she is the author of a series of photobooks entitled *Wake Up, This Is Joburg* (Fourthwall).